ATOMIC ADVISOR

by

Josh Hohenstein

DEDICATION

To my family, whose love and support have been my constant inspiration.

To the resilient financial advisors and professionals who strive to make a difference every day instead of just trying to make a buck, often at their own expense.

And to everyone who dares to dream big and persevere, even when the journey gets tough.

This book is for you.

Acknowledgments

First and foremost, I want to thank my wife, Isabella and children Scarlett, Harrison and Hendrix for their unwavering support and understanding throughout this journey. Your love and encouragement have been my greatest source of strength, and you are all the reason I have continued to strive so hard towards my dreams.

To my friends and colleagues in the financial services industry, thank you for your camaraderie, insights, and the countless discussions that have helped shape the ideas in this book. Your shared experiences and wisdom have been invaluable.

I owe a special thanks to Lee Daniels, my former partner, whose belief in me gave me the push I needed to believe, and most importantly — know that marketing was calling. Despite our journey ending in the business sense, you have been a cornerstone of my success.

To everyone I served with, from the highest ranking officers to the brand new soldiers, thank you for the foundational experiences and the lessons learned, even when they were tough. Each challenge and setback only fueled my determination to succeed.

A heartfelt thank you to the amazing people at Team Rubicon and the veterans I had the honor of working with during disaster relief efforts. Your dedication and spirit of service are truly inspiring. To Jake Wood, and Art De La Cruz, thank you for allowing this life changing experience to come into my life, I will never forget it.

I also want to acknowledge the brilliant minds whose work has influenced my approach to marketing and financial services: Seth Godin, Russell Brunson, Jim Edwards, Sabri Suby, Neil Patel, and Donald Miller. Your teachings have been a guiding light.

To my clients, thank you for trusting me with your financial journeys. Your faith in my guidance has been the driving force behind my continuous growth and innovation. You will always deserve better and more, and I will always strive to provide that to you.

To everyone who has faced rejection, setbacks, or moments of doubt, this book is for you. Keep pushing forward, embrace the journey, and know that success is within reach.

And lastly, thank you to everyone who ever told me I couldn't, or that I wasn't enough, or that I would never accomplish something that I had set my mind to. I never would have been able to appreciate the people who loved and supported me along the way if we hadn't met.

Thank you all for being a part of my story. I couldn't have done it without you.

TABLE OF CONTENT

L ike many financial advisors and professionals, I was initially drawn to the career because I believed it was an opportunity to unlock the secrets that make the world go around, and in the process, build a secure future for myself.

And like many financial advisors and professionals, I quickly realized that this profession isn't really about either of those things. It's about the impact you make in the lives of the people you guide, and for the first few years I was in the industry, I was getting it all wrong.

I thought it was what my managers and leaders told me: "It's a numbers game; just keep going and one day it will all work out." So, in the summer of 2016 with freshly minted securities and insurance licenses ready to go, I got started.

At the firm I started with, you had to go "door-knocking" to prospect for clients. Don't get me wrong, it works very well, but only if you get really good at it. So, day-in and day-out, I hit the streets in Houston, Texas. I'll share my secret tricks in a little bit, but for now, just know that I did this for over 3 months, every day. During the course of this experience in direct-to-consumer marketing at their doorstep, I learned a lot. Mostly about other human beings.

I was chased by dogs.

I was stopped by police.

I was chased by neighborhood security patrol.

I was laughed off of doorsteps.

I was told to go get a 'real job'.

A gun was pulled on me, twice.

As I stood, drenched in sweat, in the middle of the road in Kingwood, Texas, fumbling through my sweat-soaked prospecting sheet, I paused and looked up at the sky with my eyes closed.

"Is everything really this difficult?" I couldn't help but think this as my "check engine" light came on for the day, and it wasn't even noon yet.

I had been door-knocking for a couple of weeks at this point, and there were days I wished I would have taken the easy road and just stayed in the military or become a police officer or something I already knew how to do really well.

My time in the service did not make me very good at asking for help, but on this day, I was at my limits and didn't know what to do. So, I called my 'regional leader', named Aaron to get some guidance.

"Hey Josh, what's up?" he said.

I replied, "Hey Aaron! Not much, I'm just out here door-knocking and running into some troubles."

He already knew what to say, "Yeah, we all definitely have them. Here's the deal - you just keep doing it, and then eventually, it works."

"What works?" I thought, as I began to notice a very elderly man emerge from the home I had just knocked on before calling.

I freaked out and told Aaron I'd have to call him back and walked up to meet the elderly gentleman who appeared confused, mostly about who I was. So, I walked towards him, ready to make my dreams happen.

I thought, "This was it, just like Aaron said - just do it and it works." Just when he was a couple of steps away from me, I became activated with confidence. "Make it happen Josh," repeated louder and louder in my head until he was close enough to touch.

"Why the fuck are you out here knocking on people's doors? I was watching my shows," the old man sneered as soon as he came to a stop.

"Uh, I, uh... well... I'm a financial advisor and I was just out..." was all that stumbled out of my mouth before he got back on one.

"You're a financial advisor?! Knocking on people's doors? Hahaha... What is this world coming to? Sorry, I'm not trying to be rude (still chuckling), but I thought you were trying to sell me pest control or a home security system or something. Financial advisor? Y'all must be getting desperate, but hard workers are tough to come by. Say, my son has a construction business if you're looking to make more money and not be out here knocking on these doors. I can tell him about you. He'll get a kick out of it."

I replied, "I appreciate that, but I was in the Army and got out to start this, so I'll stick with it. I'm guessing you have someone already?"

He said, "Of course I have someone; everyone does. That's why knocking on these doors is silly; you're just going to meet people who have real financial advisors who have offices."

4

After a few more useless exchanges, I thanked him for his time and kept on walking.

I'm thankful I listened to my inner voice to not give up. At the time, I was much less attuned to myself and didn't know it as an inner voice, but as a rather compulsive need to succeed where others have failed. At that junction in my career, I had spent 3 weeks collecting phone numbers for 12 hours a day and had less than 50 prospective clients to show for it.

9 weeks later, I would have over 750.

During this time, I had epiphany after epiphany, and each one led me to this understanding: in order to find success in this business, you need to go find it and create it yourself. The reason everyone says, "Just keep going" is because that's what they were told and it was what they did.

Today, I would be surprised if 10% of successful financial advisors could articulate exactly how and why they built their businesses the way they did. Even fewer could provide a tangible roadmap to similar success if they had to do it again.

The first 12-18 months in the industry were a whirlwind but I was able to bring in $10 million in assets and was on my way with over 80 new and legitimate households, until Hurricane Harvey struck Houston in August of 2017. Due to some contract and compensation disputes with my firm, I quit, and took a brief hiatus from financial services, to work in disaster relief and recovery as a director of operations for a non-profit, focused on providing volunteer services with veterans.

This unlocked a whole new world for me. For the first time, I had a marketing budget, and no restrictions on how to go about it. So, I put my marketing hat on and spent tens of thousands of dollars trying to effectively market to donors and recruit veterans to the cause.

I failed time and time again with ads.

I sent ultra-spammy emails that had 15% unsubscribe rates.

I was suspended from Google Ads 3 times for doing things wrongly.

I made content, like fliers and brochures that look like what my kids made.

I designed programs that only "flew" because they were for non-profit work.

I made shaky, unfocused videos.

I wrote content and whitepapers that no one ever read.

I read everything I could from all of the popular marketers at the time, like Seth Godin, Neil Patel, and Donald Miller. I took course after course, including going to AdCon and joining the American Marketing Association.

I had been making some good strides with growth, donations, volunteer impact, and overall cohesion of my group. I was nearing the end of my original commitment when I decided that I was ready to go back into financial services, part time, to enable me build some momentum to get back in the industry. My manager said it was totally cool for me to do this.

A couple of days after I reinstated my licenses at my current firm, I was promptly summoned to a virtual call via which I was fired, as both of my children sat in my office.

"Everything is really this difficult," my mind confirmed as the flashback from my day on the street came back to me. It was now almost 3 years since I had left the Army to chase my dreams, and I found myself right back at square one.

Knowing how a 'part-time' advisor gig would work out, I had to jump back in head first. My firm, at the time, used a new process — one I eagerly presented to my former clients in attempts to accelerate my re-start up in the business.

I burned through my top 10 clients in the first week.

All of them said "no"; they wouldn't switch. None would tell me why, even though they were excited initially. It later turned out to be that the new process was in such stark difference to what I led with before, that it wasn't a fit.

Those 10 people had 80% of my asset base. I was in trouble.

For the next few months, I carried that trauma and blamed it on the firm. My bills were still going unpaid, but it felt good knowing that it wasn't my fault. However, time was running out and I had to find my footing.

One day, in 2018, as I was sitting in my office, I stumbled upon a LinkedIn automation tool that promised to send all of my messages for me; this made me feel like I had just hit the jackpot. I had consistently added LinkedIn connections for a year and had over 7,000 at this point. I could do the exact same thing I did, knocking on doors, but this time, online and automatically — this was a no brainer.

This was before the widespread of AI, so I searched online for ways to design a message sequence and got some tips before crafting my first drive to success. For a week or two, I carefully and meticulously smithed words into the catalyst that would bring about my success. After that, I set up the messages (with tons of anxiety) to start sending to my LinkedIn audience.

I launched it on a Friday with the intention of working over the weekend during regular business hours. I went home, eager to check on my results, first thing on Monday morning.

As I pulled up and refreshed my browser in my office on Monday, I couldn't believe it. People actually responded. Not just a few people; a lot of people. In the first week, I had set up over 11 appointments, and with minimal work. I would get responses like, "Yeah, Josh, give me a call xxx-xxx-xxxx" or "Sure, when can we meet?"

My eyes glazed over as I read positive feedback after positive feedback and knew this would be the future of my business. For the next 2 weeks, I would set over 30 appointments effortlessly, I was back in the game and better than before — until I wasn't.

Three weeks after my "Client Mining" discovery, everyone heard about it. I was the Wonderkid. However, the people who heard about it included my home office who informed me that my "golden egg" was a violation of their discount agreement with LinkedIn Sales Navigator and that I needed to stop. At the beginning of the day, I had over 500 messages queued up, practically guaranteed to bring in at least 50 appointments. By the end of the day, my LinkedIn dreams were dead.

I told them to cancel the agreement with LinkedIn and we could do this instead but it was a non-starter. This is when I learned that financial service firms are just as bureaucratic and poorly run as the government. It was also when I learned that no financial service firm cares about you as much as you'll care about yourself. I'd like to peg financial services with this, but let's face it — that is big business in general.

Back to square one again.

Luckily, by this time, I had drummed up enough business to keep me afloat for a bit longer, until the end of the year. That's when another financial advisor who had a lot more experience and tenure than me took an interest in what I was up to and recruited me to work exclusively on his team.

I was apprehensive to this, having always been told this was an "individual sport", and being the junior, I knew that I was just a couple of pissed off people away from being back at square one again. But with a backpack full of zero options, I leapt. This time, into the high-net-worth niche world of Dentists & Physicians. This was where I learned the value of a team, and the value of carving out my own oasis for people to gravitate towards.

We started to have some success with a Facebook group we had found with our ideal clients in droves. As I sat in meeting after meeting, learning the nuances of what made this market different, how to sell to it, and what needs to address, I also began "cutting my teeth" on less experienced doctors that had already graduated and completed residency programs. I knew the market was saturated at the front with residents, and I didn't have the 3-4 years to invest in these people before I started making money.

I had child support due, a mortgage, and several other expenses that took the luxury of time away from me. It needed to happen quickly.

As I laid out my plans to do recurring content that would help build up trust with our audience, once again, the universe spoke. The recent outbreak of COVID-19 had just shuttered businesses nationwide. As you can imagine, this threw everyone and everything into overdrive.

Our compliance department was one of a few that didn't completely collapse but it was hobbling along when it got jammed full with COVID related webinars. Turn-around time went from 1-2 weeks to 3-4 and pecking order was established by production.

I was barely at square 'two' at this point, on the precipice of falling back; something needed to happen. The more I looked at my content, the more I realized that what we needed to do was help business owners navigate PPP and EIDL provisions to keep their businesses going.

And that's when it hit me. We needed an OBA — Outside Business Activities. When done correctly, provide a new and improved methodology to go to market for a legitimate offer. An OBA is basically permission from your firm to be tied to or operate (to an extent) another business. The key factor was that it couldn't take up more than 10% of my time during trading hours. That was easy; I didn't spend any time on it. I just needed to market it, which I did after business hours anyway.

So, we teamed up with the CPA. We worked with frequently and founded the Tax Planning and Consulting firm, Exponential Equations or E2.

The breaks were off, and I put all of my accumulated marketing skills to work and put together an on-the-go webinar series that happened daily. This was where I learned how to use what I call the "Phantom Webinar". This is the kind of webinar that, if you can get your compliance officer on board with it, can change the game for you. At the back, I include a detailed guide on how to do this webinar, but for this purpose. Know that it's basically a webinar that you set up and host, but don't talk on. By becoming like a 'reporter', you have the ability to interview anyone about anything without submitting content for compliance approval. In the worst case, assuming your compliance office is amenable, you'll need to submit the registration page, the invite, and any emails you'll use if you use a sequence. Once it's over, you just submit the attendee list and you're done. By doing this, we cut a 3-4 week turn around down to 1-2 days.

We were also able to generate critical revenue during that time using the bonafide OBA with CPA support that helped us level up.

Using this methodology also enabled me to start learning and developing my marketing skills again, as this went on for a few months. I took the time to get the Professional Certified Marketer designation from the American Marketing Association, and the Certified Digital Marketing Professional designation from the Digital Marketing Institute. I even got a chance to attend a special Digital Marketing Strategy course at Harvard University.

We went from basic email sequences with some follow ups to complete client journeys with dozens of emails and targeting interests to refining into segments and more. This was just on email.

We broke from conventional wisdom, and at great risk, abandoned the all-in-one marketing tool provided to us by our firm to create everything from scratch. From custom websites, to integrations, automated webinars, niche-focused events, and custom video branding, I've had to run the marketing gauntlet.

What you're going to learn as you read is more than just some simple played out marketing tactics. I can say with relatively high confidence (90%+) that you will not have seen most of what you're about to learn.

You're not just picking this up to pick something up. You're about to experience a powerful transformation if you allow yourself to. For context, if I would have tried to write this book three or four years ago, it would have been something like "100 Marketing Things You Should Do" but through this experience, I can definitively say to you that there are far less things you should do to get you much further down the road. In this book, we'll cover the core and essential components required for any growth you could ever need.

What you'll discover is that there are less than a dozen things that if you get right, you'll never worry about getting clients, scaling effectively, or loving what you do again. The things you'll work on getting right in this book will be with you on the journey and road ahead; they're evergreen and will never go out of style.

When you're done with this strategy, it won't matter what tactics you use because who you are, what you are, and how you serve will resonate throughout time and space. I know this because I have lived it, and because of my experience, you won't need to spend the next 5 years figuring this out for yourself.

Introduction

The journey you're about to embark on is a journey of transformation, not just for your clients, but for you as well. Regardless of your attained level of success, many of you already know and realize that there is a point where money no longer serves a deep a purpose as it once did.

This is not a book about how to make more money, although I almost guarantee that you will, if you do the work contained within.

This is not a book of tricks, magic spells, hacks, or developing other-worldly abilities to place yourself upon a pedestal as the "special one" — the one who knows all, or is better or more worthy of the journey they lead others on.

This is a book of realization. The work you will endeavor to accomplish here will be difficult at first, because you may think that the work is too hard or you see yourself as

15

unworthy and incapable. This would only be true when you believe that you are not the person that you see unfold before you while doing this work. You may believe you cannot ever become this person, others are more worthy, qualified or deserving of being the person you want to become.

This is a fallacy because the work contained within this book is not about 'becoming' as much as it is about 'being' and realizing that you actually already are the person that unfolds before you. All you need to do is accept it as true, and begin to live your life in the way the person you see would. It's that simple. The problem begins with knowing we are human, and with humans, things are seldom simple, so we seek complexity to satisfy our need.

"If it were so simple, why doesn't everyone do it?"

Getting in shape is simple. Building a business can be simple. Your relationships can be simple. Most things can be simplified and still maintain their original value. It's through the human need to create complexity that the issues arise.

The primary objective of the work contained in this book is to help you transform your complex, difficult-to-navigate, and impossible-to-quantify offer with intangible promises into an accessible (simple) and irresistible (clear) offer. By the end of this book, you can achieve both.

When Simplicity Works:

Post-Its

In the late 1960s, Spencer Silver, a scientist at 3M, discovered a unique adhesive that could stick to surfaces yet be easily removed without leaving residue. Despite the adhesive's potential, Silver struggled to find a practical use for it. Enter Art Fry, a colleague who needed a bookmark that wouldn't slip out of his hymn book during choir practice. Fry had an epiphany and used Silver's adhesive to create the Post-It Note. This simple, yet ingenious solution revolutionized office work and personal organization, demonstrating how straightforward ideas can have a monumental impact.

iPhones

Before the iPhone's debut in 2007, smartphones were cluttered with complicated menus and numerous buttons. Steve Jobs envisioned a device that was intuitive and easy to use. By eliminating the keyboard and introducing a touch screen with a single home button, Apple transformed the mobile phone industry. The iPhone's simplicity made it accessible to millions, proving that reducing complexity can lead to groundbreaking innovation.

Automobiles

Henry Ford revolutionized the automobile industry with the introduction of the assembly line in 1913. Before this innovation, cars were handcrafted by skilled workers in a slow, expensive process. Ford's vision was to simplify production by dividing the work into simple, repetitive tasks performed by unskilled labor. This not only sped up manufacturing but also made cars affordable to the masses. Ford's approach exemplifies how simplifying complex processes can lead to extraordinary advancements.

When Complexity Doesn't

Concorde Jet

The Concorde was an engineering marvel — a supersonic passenger jet that could cross the Atlantic in record time. Despite its speed and technological prowess, the Concorde was too complex and expensive to operate. Its high operating costs, noise restrictions, and limited seating capacity led to its eventual retirement. A simpler, more efficient approach to air travel, like the Boeing 787 Dreamliner, which focuses on fuel efficiency and passenger comfort, has proven to be more sustainable and commercially successful.

NASA Pen

During the space race, NASA spent millions developing a pen that could write in zero gravity, under extreme temperatures, and on almost any surface. Meanwhile, the Soviet space program opted for a simpler solution: they used pencils. The complex and costly development of the "space pen" serves as a reminder that sometimes, simple solutions are not only more cost-effective but also more efficient.

Healthcare.gov Launch

When Healthcare.gov launched in 2013, it was meant to be a simple way for Americans to sign up for health insurance under the Affordable Care Act. However, the website was plagued with technical issues due to its overly complex design and poor project management. Users experienced crashes, long wait times, and incorrect information. A more straightforward, phased approach could have ensured a smoother rollout, allowing for troubleshooting and adjustments before a full-scale launch.

Windows Vista

Microsoft's Windows Vista was intended to be a groundbreaking operating system with a host of new features and a complex security system. However, its complexity led to widespread compatibility issues, slow performance, and a confusing user interface. Consumers and businesses alike were frustrated, leading many to stick with or revert to Windows XP. Microsoft learned from this and opted for a more streamlined and user-friendly approach with Windows 7, which was much better received.

Did you notice the patterns in these overly complex failures compared to more simplistic success stories? You can go back and analyze if you want to, but the answer lies in who the solution was created for — who was considered at the top of the hearts and minds when this creation came to life.

In their successes, their simple designs were focused purely on the users of the product or service. The iPhone provided an effortless and inexpensive solution to remembering important things. It also made a world of complex and confusing technology easy to use, and the assembly line made the automobile less expensive and faster to make, so that more people could have access to them.

In the failures, their complex designs were focused purely on the ideation, beliefs, and philosophies of major corporations who believed (incorrectly) that they knew exactly what their customers wanted, so they didn't need to ask them.

The first simple lesson in this book is to make your offer accessible to everyone — those who are ready, those who aren't, those who are still kicking the tires, and even those who have said "no".

The second simple lesson in this book is to make your offer irresistible to the right people, and intolerable to the wrong people.

To make your offer like this, you need to understand that everything we'll discuss about this is "outside of the box", meaning you will not do this work with what you currently know today. What you currently know today is a world of compliance and people being so terrified of getting in trouble that it feels easier to just take what they can get.

If you take what you can get, you're only ever going to get the same thing as everyone else. There are over 250,000 financial professionals in the United States alone and over 245,000 are in the "take what you can get" bucket.

The other 5,000 are in the "get exactly what I want" bucket, and this is the bucket I want you to get into. By doing this work, you can achieve that.

To better understand what's "outside of the box" in this process, we should first explore what is "inside of the box" and that is your "custom" or "unique" 5-step process used to sell things to people. For most professionals, even very successful ones, that played-out process is usually more like:

1) Step One: Initial meeting and financial discovery

2) Step Two: Some sort of commitment to a financial plan for a fee, moving investment accounts, or getting underwritten for insurance.

3) Step 3, 4, and 5 are probably written down and marketed, but the truth is that once the money making events have occurred, you'll get ready to move on to the next and your clients will still be waiting around for the eventual delivery of the

experience you promised. The experience, however, never comes, and as you continue to grow, the ones who helped you get to where you are fade from John and Jane to Account #ABC12345678.

For the record, it's not your fault — the dynamics of the industry position all of us to put making money before anything else when we get started. It's also why we have so many problems with behavior in our industry, but that's for another day.

Just know that if this is what you're doing, you are about to benefit tremendously from this text because you won't be doing this much longer. You won't be selling things to people who barely have the ability to transact and exchange value with you. You won't be panning for golden scraps in the streams, and you won't be making promises that you know you won't deliver on.

I can say all of this to you because I've been there; I've done it. I've been that financial advisor, and if I could go back and do it all over again, I probably would because it took me to this point where I can serve as your guide on the journey ahead, but I can help to ensure that you never have to ask yourself that question.

In many ways, this book is about so much more than marketing. By the end, you will know more about marketing yourself and your brand as a financial advisor than 99% of the profession, but most importantly, you will know how to put all of the information into action in your life.

Like many books, this text will build upon itself, but unlike other books, this is not a series of anecdotes and interviews with famous people to build credibility; it's not a treasure bag of 'golden nuggets' for you to randomly apply in your practice. It is a framework and recipe that takes you to the top of the mountain where you may shine your light for all to see.

You may skip aspects of this text, and the work contained, but your light will not shine as brightly as it needs to. The good news is that if you scale this mountain too quickly to see the meaningful results you desire, you may descend to overlooked points on your journey to learn the lesson and re-ascend back to the top.

So, here we go — it's time to take you up the mountain.

Let's go.

1

SOLVE THE 3 ADVISOR DILEMMAS

- Who am I?
- What am I?
- How do I serve?

About a year after leaving the Army, I was able to make a fast start for myself in the financial services industry. I had opened my office near where I grew up, I had knocked on over 5,000 doors walking the streets of Houston, Texas, and thought that everything was falling into place as I had imagined it. I didn't know it then, but I was really sitting in the "eye of the storm" and enjoying a relatively calm period in my life before a lot of upheaval would occur.

Right around a year into building my practice, Hurricane Harvey struck and left a bustling metropolis home to millions of people looking more like a swamp than a city. Initially, I was concerned about my clients, and then my business. I couldn't get ahold of anyone, which was expected, but it didn't help my anxiousness subside much as I speculated what it would be like to go back to square one in the blink of an eye.

What made it worse was the guilt of the impact on me. For whatever reason, I still had electricity, running water, and hardly felt the impacts of the hurricane directly. Less than 1,000 feet away, on the other side of the highway, entire communities were literally half underwater, and millions of people were displaced.

I was still relatively conditioned to military life after spending nearly a decade in service to our country and there was just this nagging feeling that kept coming up. As I watched the real time updates during the first few hours after Harvey struck, I began to feel a compulsion to act.

"You know who you are; you are capable, and this is what you do. Why are you sitting here still?"

The thought came back over and over during the next hour and I was paralyzed, but not from fear. It was the duality of who I thought that I was that was in conflict. I had left military life behind. I had been very lucky and blessed to come back after multiple deployments in infantry units with relatively few injuries — at least compared to what it could have been. I was now supposed to be in a new life phase, and financial advisors aren't supposed to go put themselves in danger to help people. I felt that first responders were better equipped to deal with this, and I would be happy to support in other ways.

Convincing myself to not go out and do anything became more of an exercise, but it didn't last very long. Before the news segment had ended, I received a call from my executive assistant's brother.

"Hey man, I know you're probably dealing with all this craziness right now in Houston, but Jodie mentioned that the office was closed. Well, I have a boat and I was going to head into the city and see if I could lend a hand. I thought since you were in the military, you might be open to coming along with me so that we don't get lost."

I didn't hesitate.

"When are you going to be here?" I asked eagerly, already forgetting the identity crisis I had just experienced.

"About 3 hours. I'm leaving right now but the roads are iffy, so I'll have to take some backroads. Can I call you when I'm close?" he inquired.

I said, "Sure, I'll get my things ready now and we'll head out as soon as you get here."

By the time he arrived, I had just gotten back from helping set up a few hundred cots at the George R. Brown convention center, and after grabbing a few things (mostly snacks), we headed out into the sunken city to see what difference we could make.

After over 2 days of performing evacuations for stranded Houstonians by boat, we experienced the event that would change everything. A boat carrying 8 police officers came careening down what once was a road for cars to drive on, and quickly became ensnared in low hanging trees. Despite their best efforts to free the vessel, they only had about 30 seconds before the boat capsized and ejected all of them into the water.

They were wearing life vests, so being in the water was not the issue. It was the fact that currents were running 15 to 20 miles per hour in places that water should not be. This left substantial debris underneath, like fallen trees, abandoned vehicles, collapsed or broken-off infrastructure that could easily grab anyone and pull them down to their demise. This was only part of the gauntlet, because if they were pulled into the open waters in Lake Houston, there was no one between them and the Gulf of Mexico that could respond in time.

We acted quickly and maneuvered our boat behind a female police officer holding on to a tree. The current was so strong that she was parallel to the surface of the water, almost as if she was floating on it. As we pulled up, I yelled, "Don't let go; we're coming up!" I'm not sure what she heard, but as soon as I shouted that, she let go.

What happened next was even quicker. She barely had time to turn around and face the boat in the water before she started to go underneath it. Just for you to understand the power of this water, we were in a small fishing boat designed for lakes with a 250cc outboard engine at full throttle, and we were fighting to maintain our position in the water without being pushed back.

Given my military training, I remembered that body armor has a drag handle positioned at the back-top to help them be dragged in the event that they're too wounded to move. Instantly, I shoved my arm into the water, hoping to grab something solid before she inevitably went to the back of the boat, right where the engine was pushing, full throttle.

I still believe it was fate — or something else — that intervened, because my hand grabbed exactly where that handle was. As soon as I secured my grip, I joined her trajectory and began to slide and get pulled off the boat. My boat mate, Jonathon, couldn't get off the wheel to come grab me or face the risk of losing control of the boat, and for a brief moment, I thought about letting go. As soon as I did, I looked down into the water and just 6 inches below the surface of the water, I could see her face looking up at me. It is still strange to me to this day, but her face was completely calm, as if she knew that I was going to pull her up, and she was merely waiting for me to do so. So, that's what I did. I slowly stood up until she could get her head above water and secure a grip on the boat, so that I could pull her in.

It felt like we wrestled with the currents and the weight of her water-logged gear for 30 minutes, although I'm sure it was only one or two. Finally, she was able to pull one of her legs up on the side of the boat and I was able to pull her in. As we laid on the floor of the front of the boat, we looked up at the grey overcast skies as Jonathon fought the currents to get her to a drop-off point at the nearby bridge that had only a short window before it would become flooded.

As we recovered and found a place to sit, the adrenaline was wearing off and I began to feel a searing pain in my shoulder. I knew it was probably dislocated but I tried to appear unphased as we neared our final approach to the bridge.

Before she got off, I asked her for her name. "Melanie," she replied. "It was nice to meet you Melanie," I responded calmly as I shook her hand and helped her off the boat.

We continued on our mission for the remainder of the day. It was filled with some narrowly missed disasters, with one resulting in our boat crashing head-first into a restaurant — with 5 other people on board — and then through the other side of the restaurant. We just kept going like nothing happened and dropped them off at the bridge before it became flooded a few minutes later.

In the weeks and months after this event, I was featured on the news quite often, mostly because I captured the boat overturning on video. This happened because I was filming the ridiculously long line of boats we were in, waiting to get into a senior living community to pick up passengers to take to safety. Consequently, I got messages of gratitude from Melanie, her husband (also a police officer), and their family. It turned out that she was pregnant at the time of the rescue, and saving her life resulted in the welcoming of a child into their life.

In February, following the devastating events, I was honored by the City of Houston and Houston Police Department with the Life Saving Public Service Award, which was quite a difficult thing to accept; I was just in the right place at the right time. I felt so weird about it that I didn't even tell my family it was going on, which also included my time visiting news stations. In many instances, I got calls and messages while I was on the news from very disgruntled family members.

It's not that it was weird for me; it felt like that was who I was. The thought of what this family would have had to go through by losing a daughter, wife, and soon-to-be mother still shook me though. I was only glad that I did what I did so that I could prevent the tragedy I imagined in my mind from unfolding.

After this experience, and within 4 months, I left the financial services industry. I took an opportunity to serve as a deputy director of operations for a veteran-based non-profit organization called Team Rubicon which focused on providing volunteer disaster relief efforts in the immediate aftermath of catastrophic events.

During my year there, despite my similarities with everyone in the organization, like military service, a passion for helping, and commitment to a better world, I felt out of place. I felt like it was wrong for me to be there — like I didn't belong.

I thought about this a lot and one day, I was browsing some old content from the organization as I prepared to create a presentation to pitch to a Fortune 500 company for donations, I discovered the basis of the concept I'll share with you in this chapter.

Right there, on the slide, it read, "The Key to Resilience & Helping Veterans Live Fulfilled Lives". Just below the headline were three circles arranged in a triangle shape, each containing a single word — Identity, Community, and Purpose. My intuition made me dig deeper into this, and the more I read it, the more it made sense — for veterans, yes, but most importantly, for ALL people.

All people need to understand their identity — who they are.

All people need to know what value they add to the community — what they are.

All people need to know their purpose for impacting their community — how they serve.

Knowing these three things doesn't only provide immense clarity on your journey, it makes you resilient to every adverse impact that comes your way. This is because there is a difference between the things we "think" and the things we "know". When we are in what I call our "knowing", answers come to us very easily.

In my knowing, I instantly understood within minutes after reading that slide deck that I didn't feel like I belonged, because I didn't. I was meant for something else. I am meant to serve and guide others on some of the toughest journeys that they can take, but I had gotten what I was and how I served wrongly because I was thinking about what I should do instead of knowing what I should do.

The part of you that knows, is your soul, or your essence, or spirit — whatever you want to call it. You are here for a much bigger purpose than you can possibly imagine.

Whether you realize it or not, your soul is asking you to answer this, nearly every day. It already knows the answer but it wants you to say it. All the work here is designed to create clarity for this. When you know who you are, what you are, and how you serve, this work would become easy. Until you do (this may illuminate) you will find it very hard to attract, connect, and convert clients.

Your on-hand skills might get you a ways down the road but I promise that without these, at some point, you will break down, and in the best case, fall very short of your potential without understanding how you got there.

So, if you are not ready to know who and what you are as well as how you serve, you may close this book until you are. If you attempt to move forward without this clarity, you will become lost and frustrated with no clear path home. This is your choice to make, and experience through.

So, then. Who are you? You may know yourself as John or Jane, a man or woman, young or old but those have nothing to do with who you are. Those are ways of identifying through personality, through what we have ascribed to ourselves, or allowed to be ascribed to us.

The first step in knowing who you are is knowing who you are not, and that is whatever you have been led to believe you are, for better or worse.

For most of us, we've been told our entire lives what has value, what doesn't , what's good vs. bad, who is worthy or not, who deserves what they get, and on and on…

Our entire world is codified with labels that require us to not have to stop and figure everything out, or anything out. But what if all the labels are incorrect? How would the world change if everyone realized this?

Instead of speculating, imagine it. Look at everything in your room, your house, your car, or even the things you wear.

Some of those things cost X or took Y to get, which makes them Z compared to A…

Yes, those things.

Now take all of the labels, statuses, covetousness, rarities, mental tags and categories and remove them; even a name is a label.

Look at all of those things again and just see them for what they are — things that other people who came before you said. No matter the 'thing', I can promise you with certainty that it will not be here 100 years from now; not in its current state, anyway.

So, you must accept that you will live in a world of impermanence, where nothing that is today, will be forever.

The lens you have lived your life through has served you enough to arrive here at the doorstep of transformation, and now your choice is to walk up the steps and knock on the door to see the real you open the door and invite you in. Imagine it if you can.

As you imagine walking in, take notice of how you feel. For many of you, it will feel inexplicably warm and light, almost like wavelengths of love become imbued with who you are.

The you that is inside, is the real you. The you on the steps is who you have been convinced you are. The mission of this chapter is for you to understand this more deeply than you have ever understood anything.

You are one with the source — the vibrational frequency of love, the universe, God, Allah, the Monad, whatever you wish to know it as. Without labels, it can only be known as you.

Now, I may have just frightened you, thinking you got a marketing book to trick you into a religious conversation, but we are and will remain very far from it as we continue.

What I am revealing to you is not religious, but it is holy. Despite the workings of our world to keep us within the shackles of fear and control, I am here to deliver this message to you. You are free, you are free, you are free – and a true message is always true regardless of the messenger.

Free to do what? To be your own divine light. To know that you have always been a perfect creation — an aspect of the source from the very day you arrived here. You have just forgotten and otherwise convinced by all of your perceptions about who you are.

So, who you are is the light. Just as I shine my own light from where I am on the mountain to guide you up, you will do the same for your clients. To do this, you may say to yourself now:

"I know who I am"

Now that you understand who you are, it's time to know what you are. If you are the light, then what you are is a beacon, a portal if you prefer, to helping others know who and what they are as well.

You are not a messiah, or prophet – everyone is. Do you understand this? What you are is an example of what others can become at the level of the soul. Just by being you in your light, you can transform everything.

I don't think I need to explain further how powerful this will be when interacting with another person seeking a guide on their Journey and now you may say:

"I know what I am"

Finally, you must know how you serve. To do this, you must also know that you are healing people.

Most of the financial work you do with clients will be emotional and most of what you guide them to do will be to overcome those emotions that tell them to do something that might hurt them and cause them to fall into a hole that's 20 feet deeper.

You aren't starting a cult or religion, and there will not be any KoolAid to drink at the end.

You are using finances as a conduit for greater transformational change, the holistic improvement and betterment of every life you touch. You're creating a movement, a cause, and a revolution from darkness to light, guiding others to you and through you in order for them to realize who they are as well.

To make this happen, you may say this aloud or to yourself.

- I know who I am
- I know what I am
- I know how I serve

You may align to this frequency at any time by saying this. It doesn't matter where you are or if you say it out loud or to yourself.

Now that we have arrived at this knowing, it's time to build an unstoppable brand. Knowing who and what you are, and how you serve allows you to move into the specificity of what hero you will seek to guide.

As an example, think about this book. The content could easily have been made to apply to all solopreneur or service businesses — but why isn't it? Because of my affinity. I am also a financial advisor. I can deeply relate to the specific challenges you face because I have climbed that mountain before.

Just like a highly skilled sherpa, 100 summits on Mt. Everest doesn't necessarily qualify them to guide people up k2 or Kilimanjaro. It is because I have climbed your mountain that I am best equipped to guide you.

Just as this is true for me and you, it's true for you and your clients too.

Despite what I know, I could not become the guide to most clients, even your clients. Even though I am guiding you up this mountain, you have climbed another many times before and this is your domain of mastery. So, Master Sherpa, what mountain are you uniquely qualified to guide others up? In financial services, this is your niche. But let's be clear about one thing — a segment is not a niche. So, HNW people, business owners, new families, recently divorced, job changers and more are going to be removed from your vocabulary.

To elevate this and specify this initially is to view your market more in detail, and the rest of this text is about tailoring everything to make your offer as accessible and irresistible as you can to the 'right' people, your people.

Here's a good start, but we'll refine this much more as we continue.

- African American Business owners with 2+ partners, 25 years in business, revenue $1M+

- HNW LGBTQ couples with dual incomes, 2+ children, $1M investable assets

- Military doctors and dentists separating <2 years, transitioning careers

- Youtubers with 100K+ subscribers and growth focused with $100,000+ annual income

Once you figure out exactly who you want to serve, in order to build a movement or community – you need to stand for something.

It can be hard in this industry to do that. We're bombarded with suitability, best interest, and compliance requirements so much that it's almost like the life gets sucked out of you and people are so afraid to say anything, that they say nothing.

I'll say it again, "stand for something."

If you believe protection comes first, or cash flow, debt, or investing, then stand by it. If you have a valid reason not to use or recommend certain products, stand by it.

If you believe that other companies are evil, stand by it. Don't go out of your way to trash them, but do not say something you don't believe either. Nearly every aspect of this method is built upon and based on your authentic character.

Now, to truly stand in your light for others will require you to sharpen your insights and focus your light to guide others all the way down the path.

This means you need to know your stuff. Whatever your focus is, don't skip any development, even outside development. Become obsessed with improvement.

Here's what I mean, and we'll use the examples from before:

If you work with business owners, you should develop your understanding in:

- 20-30 most commonly used tax deductions and how to spot opportunities

- All tax return types and schedules including how they work together
- Reviewing Profit/Loss and other statements (QB or other)
- Basic tax implications of business sale
- Basic legal entity structure design (pros/cons)
- A content creator business is different from HVAC – dig deeper

If you lead with a particular focus, like college planning

- Know how the financial aid arena works, from FAFSA to loans
- Know how scholarships work and how to find them
- Know how state specific benefits and federal grants work
- Know how military benefits work
- Know what the financial picture should look like to qualify for aid

If you're focusing on a particular market or community

- Deeply understand the financial problems faced by them

- Find financial resource and other knowledge hubs specific to them

- Learn how to build an online community to support them

- Know the average childhood and upbringing culturally

I want to be clear about something, when you create your niche, it's your experiences that qualify you, not how or what you look like or identify as.

For example, with my experiences in the Army in the Middle East, I was very deeply exposed to Islamic culture. To build trust and rapport, we often honored cultural traditions when meeting local leaders, and because of that, I learned a lot about it.

If I were to deeply educate myself about the Islamic financial mindset, it could be totally possible for me as a flaxen haired, blue eyed, white man to have a niche focused on serving an Islamic faith base.

Most would think that's silly, but speaking globally, there are many people all over the world who practice Islam and look very much like me, particularly in areas between Russia and the Middle East.

When I approach this market with a truly special offer, I become competitive, even more than an advisor who is actually Islamic and only markets to that aspect, without the offer.

As we close this chapter, you should already feel the shift happening. You know who and what you are, and how you serve, and before moving to the next, start here because there's still more to do. We'll need to eat this elephant one bite at a time, and your first bite is below:

Instructions: When completing this exercise, you should not use products or services that you already know. Your focus is about helping people — what qualifies you is about you as a person, and your areas of mastery are things you must learn to fulfill the first two promises.

Who Am I?

My specialty focus is:

_____

_____

_____

_____

_____

_____

_____

_____

_____

_____

_____

_____

_____

_____

Framework: My specialty is in helping X (hero identity) people do Y (aspirational goal), so that they can Z (good thing), without V (bad thing).

Example: My specialty is in helping financial advisors (hero identity) build authentic connections with their clients (aspirational goal), so they can enjoy a thriving practice with loyal clients and steady referrals (good thing), without the stress of navigating intricate and confusing marketing tactics (bad thing).

What qualifies me to guide:

_____

_____

_____

_____

_____

_____

_____

_____

_____

_____

_____

_____

_____

_____

Framework: *I am qualified to guide my hero because (shared hardship and experience), and have successfully (overcome challenges and achieved their aspirational goal already). I deeply understand the nuances of their main challenges (main hero* *challenges in achieving goals on their own) and know the right way to help them achieve it (faster/safer/better/etc)*

Example: *I am qualified to guide my hero because I've experienced, firsthand, the struggles of a financial advisor trying to retain clients and manage complex marketing tactics, and have successfully turned my practice around by focusing on genuine client relationships, leading to higher retention and more referrals. I deeply understand the nuances of their main challenges, like navigating the competitive landscape and the stress of overly complicated marketing, and know the right way to help them achieve it by streamlining their client interaction and marketing processes.*

My areas of mastery are:

_____

_____

_____

_____

_____

_____

_____

_____

_____

_____

_____

_____

_____

_____

_____

Framework: *The areas I must always work to master to be the most impactful guide to my hero are (Mastery Area 1, Mastery Area 2, Mastery Area 3).*

Example: *The areas I must always work to master to be the most impactful guide to my hero are building genuine connections with clients, creating accessible and irresistible offers, and translating intricate marketing strategies into straightforward, actionable steps.*

What Am I?

What mission are you on? [The more philosophical, the better]:

_____

_____

_____

_____

_____

_____

_____

_____

_____

_____

_____

_____

_____

_____

Framework: *My mission is to [mission statement]. This mission is rooted in [philosophical belief], aiming to [impact or change you want to see in the world].*

Example: *My mission is to empower financial advisors to build deeper, more authentic relationships with their clients. This mission is rooted in the belief that genuine human connections are the cornerstone of a successful and fulfilling practice, aiming* *to transform the financial industry into a more empathetic and client-centered field.*

How do you intend to shape the world? [The more audacious, the better]:

_____

_____

_____

_____

_____

_____

_____

_____

_____

_____

_____

_____

_____

Framework: *I intend to shape the world by [audacious goal]. Through [specific actions or initiatives], I will [intended impact or change in the world].*

Example: *I intend to shape the world by redefining how financial services are delivered. Through innovative training programs and simplified marketing strategies, I will ensure that financial advisors can provide more personalized and effective guidance, making financial security and growth accessible to everyone.*

Why do you do this? [This dually serves as your backstory]:

_____

_____

_____

_____

_____

_____

_____

_____

_____

_____

_____

_____

_____

_____

Framework: I do this because *[personal backstory or motivation]*. *Having [personal experience or challenge], I [realization or lesson learned], which drives me to [current mission and goals].*

Example: I do this because I've been in the trenches as a financial advisor, struggling to keep up with complex marketing tactics and feeling disconnected from my clients. Having faced the burnout and frustration that comes from a lack of genuine client relationships, I realized that success in this industry comes from simplicity and authenticity. This drives me to help other financial advisors avoid the same pitfalls and build thriving, meaningful practices.

How Do I Serve?

What journey are you guiding others on? [Linked to the hero's aspirational goals and dreams]:

_____

_____

_____

      '

_____

_____

_____

_____

_____

_____

_____

_____

_____

_____

_____

Framework: *The journey I am guiding others on is [describe the journey]. This journey is designed to help [hero identity] achieve [aspirational goals and dreams] by [method or approach]. Along the way, they will [key milestones or transformations] and ultimately [end result or final transformation].*

Example: *The journey I am guiding others on is one of transformation, from overwhelmed financial advisors to* *confident, client-centered professionals. This journey is designed to help financial advisors achieve a thriving practice with loyal clients and steady referrals by building authentic relationships and simplifying their marketing strategies. Along the way, they will learn to connect deeply with clients, craft irresistible offers, streamline their business operations, and ultimately enjoy a more fulfilling and successful career in the financial industry.*

2

KNOW YOUR HERO

Now that who you are in your light is realized and understood; it is time to deeply know the heroes you will be guiding on their journey. To do this, we need to know both the qualitative and quantitative ways we need to connect with them. More time, effort, and attention should be put towards this, if once you're complete it doesn't align with the work from the previous section, rework both until they do, but your hero should change minimally.

Before we start, it's crucial to grasp the fundamental drivers of human behavior and what compels us to connect with some people but not others. Understanding these core motivators is key to transforming how you relate to your clients. This insight will help you forge deep, meaningful connections and become the guide they can't resist following.

Let's dive into what really makes us tick and why simplicity in these relationships is so powerful.

Let's consider the story of David, one of my clients, a financial advisor with over a decade of experience. David had all the technical knowledge and skills one could ask for, but he was struggling to build a loyal client base. His clients were constantly churning, and referrals were practically non-existent. Despite his best efforts, his business was stagnating, and he couldn't figure out why.

When David and I first met, he was skeptical about changing his approach. He was deeply rooted in the belief that clients made decisions purely based on logic and data. Behavioral biases such as confirmation bias and the status quo bias were holding him back. He believed that as long as he provided the best financial advice, clients would naturally stay loyal. This belief, however, was not aligning with his reality.

During our sessions, I introduced David to the principles of behavioral finance. We discussed how heuristics and biases like loss aversion, anchoring, and the availability heuristic affect client decisions. David was initially resistant, anchored in his ways, but gradually began to see how these biases were influencing his clients' behaviors.

For instance, David had a client who was overly conservative with investments due to a strong aversion to loss. Despite

David's logical presentations showing potential gains, the client was stuck, unable to move forward. We worked on addressing these fears directly, using empathetic communication and relatable stories to ease the client's concerns.

David also had to overcome his own status quo bias. He had a fixed mindset that changing his approach would alienate his existing clients. However, I encouraged him to test new strategies with a small subset of clients first. This gradual approach helped mitigate his fears of change.

As David started implementing these insights, the transformation was remarkable. He shifted his focus from just delivering data to understanding his clients' personal stories, fears, and aspirations. He simplified complex financial concepts and aligned his advice with the individual values and goals of his clients.

Quantifying the results, David saw a 40% increase in client retention within the first year of making these changes. His referral rate doubled, as satisfied clients began to recommend his services to friends and family. Revenue grew by 25%, as clients invested more confidently, feeling truly understood and valued.

David's story is not unique, and you can start to see that what I am suggesting to you is not some sort of inventive or novel approach to some unknown place. It's the roadmap to creating the life you've always dreamed of.

The Secret to This Approach

The place to now begin is a powerful insight from renowned marketer, Blair Warren's *One Sentence Persuasion Course*. You can learn more about it from the back of this book where I provide a link to his work, but here's how it goes:

"People will do anything for those who *encourage* their dreams, *justify* their failures, *allay* their fears, *confirm* their suspicions, and *help throw rocks* at their enemy."

Really quickly, it's not gaslighting. You are not saying anything untrue; you are focusing your communication on things they actually care about and disregarding the rest.

It's not apathy, where you don't care and are playing pretend. You're focusing your care on the things they care about, not what you care about.

Some of you may still resist this, but remember three things, I know who I am, what I am, and how I serve. You will face great difficulty trying to give someone what they want and need while making anything about yourself. You will experience the benefits as a result of the process, not as a result of the offer. Let's dive deeper.

At the basic level humans are always trying to do two things:

Survive and Thrive → Translated into motivators → Fear/scarcity and Acceptance/safety

To communicate effectively to these primal motivators, you must know specifically what fear they seek to avoid and what abundance they desire. To know this definitively, it's very helpful to understand, in the end, what all humans desire:

- To be loved
- To be in a community
- To have purpose
- To progress forward
- To make a difference

This is attainable by you, and your clients and the only reason we all do not have it is because of the things we believe that tell us that we are not worthy.

You will be the agent of change not just for yourself, but for every life you impact.

Can you understand your power now? More so, can you understand the responsibility you now have?

The final component to understand is that life's A to Z is not linear like it might be on financial projections. You can't tie a hypothetical rate of return to a person and say, "See! You're 9.45% better this year; in 20 years, you'll be a completely different person!"

So, you aren't helping people grow; you're helping them transform, from who they are, into who they want to be.

How do we pass this seemingly impossible test? Get the answers to the questions before we take the test, and this requires some research. Through this process, you'll define the preliminary avatar that you will continue to refine over your career.

You may not know the answers to everything yet, but in time you will — this book serves as a guide you can write in and reference anytime.

- What are their hopes and dreams? These should be aspirational, big goals, best case scenarios – the budding entrepreneur who wants an empire, the DIY investor who wants to have it all figured out, the parents who paid 100% of their child's college. It's not your job to validate or invalidate these. If they want to become a dinosaur, you can feel free to add some realism, otherwise, focus on who they think they should become — they can always adapt it later with your help, guidance, and love.

- What are they afraid of? Fear's purpose is only and will only ever be to create more fear. By deeply knowing this, you serve as a beacon to allay these fears, so that they can take action. These fears are deep-rooted and very personal – so, get real here.

Intangible Fear: I want to make sure I don't run out of money.

Tangible Fear: I'm afraid that despite my best efforts, we won't have enough. As the sole income earner, it's my job to make sure this doesn't fail, and if it does, it will come at my expense. I let my family down and wish I could do it another way. I don't want to involve my spouse in this because I'm afraid they will judge me for what I've done or not.

Intangible Fear: My CPA said I should watch out for these.

Tangible Fear: I like the idea of this and it makes sense but my CPA said not to. I'm afraid that if I ignore them and I'm wrong, I could be set back way more. I'm also worried if that happens, my CPA won't help me fix it. The idea of getting this wrong is worse than getting some tax savings.

Intangible Fear: I'm concerned that you're just going to try to sell me something I don't need.

Tangible Fear: I've heard so many conflicting things; I still don't know what's true. I'm worried that I'll get convinced to get something that's bad for me or something someone will judge me for doing. The potential setbacks are huge; it's probably best not to do anything.

You can see that by exploring the mind of your hero, you unlock new insights to address and new angles to approach the problems from.

For an effective Start, try to identify 3 common intangible fears for your hero and make them tangible. As always, I've provided a framework for you here before your exercise:

Framework:

1. **Identify the Intangible Fear**: Begin by pinpointing the broad, vague fear that the client has.

2. **Understand the Root Causes**: Dig deeper into the reasons behind this fear.

3. **Contextualize with Real-Life Scenarios**: Provide specific examples or scenarios where this fear might play out.

4. **Clarify the Consequences**: Explain the potential negative outcomes of this fear in a tangible way.

5. **Validate the Fear**: Acknowledge that the fear is valid and that many people share it.

6. **Provide Assurance and Solutions**: Offer clear, practical steps to address and mitigate this fear.

Example:

1. Identify the Intangible Fear: "I'm concerned you're just going to try to sell me something I don't need."

2. Understand the Root Causes: Dig deeper into why the client feels this way. Perhaps they've had bad experiences with pushy sales tactics in the past or have heard negative stories from friends and family.

3. Contextualize with Real-Life Scenarios: Provide specific examples of how this fear can manifest. For instance, "You might have heard conflicting advice about financial products, leaving you unsure about what's genuinely beneficial for you."

4. Clarify the Consequences: Explain the tangible outcomes of this fear. "This uncertainty can lead to feeling overwhelmed and making decisions based on pressure, rather than sound judgment. You might worry about being judged by others for a choice that turns out to be less than ideal, or worse, you could end up with a product that doesn't suit your needs and potentially causes financial setbacks."

5. Validate the Fear: Acknowledge the client's fear and reassure them that it's a common concern. "I understand this fear completely. Many people feel this way, especially when dealing with complex financial decisions. It's perfectly normal to feel cautious about making a significant financial commitment."

6. Provide Assurance and Solutions: Offer steps to mitigate the fear and build trust. "My goal is to help you make the best decision for your unique situation. Here's how we can help to ensure you get what you truly need:

- **Transparency**: I will provide clear, straightforward information about all available options.

- **Education**: We'll go over each option together, so that you can understand the benefits and drawbacks.

- **Customized Solutions**: I'll tailor recommendations to fit your specific goals and needs, ensuring they align with your values and long-term plans.

- **Ongoing Support**: I'm here to answer any questions and adjust the plan as your needs evolve.

Turned into Tangible Fear:

"I've heard so many conflicting things; I still don't know what's true. I'm worried I'll get convinced to buy something that's not right for me, or worse, that I'll make a decision that others will judge me for. The potential setbacks are huge, and I'm afraid it's probably best not to do anything at all."

By following this framework, you can help clients articulate their fears more concretely, making it easier to address and alleviate their concerns.

What's the hero's #1 intangible fear?

_____

_____

_____

_____

_____

_____

What's the hero's #1 tangible fear?

_____

_____

_____

_____

_____

_____

What's the hero's #2 intangible fear?

_____

_____

_____

_____

_____

_____

What's the hero's #2 tangible fear?

_____

_____

_____

_____

_____

_____

What's the hero's #3 intangible fear?

_____

_____

_____

_____

_____

_____

_____

What's the hero's #3 tangible fear?

_____

_____

_____

_____

_____

_____

To further help your design here, you'll want to expand your understanding of your hero down to the behavioral level.

This work is never ending, so I will unfold the map so that you can see what I mean as we continue, but always, always, always remember that the map is not all of the territory.

Marketing successfully is when the art and the science intersect perfectly for your brand. Everyone's special mix is special to them and their brand — yours will be too.

The categories we're about to explore amount to more than just a qualitative knowing of who you serve. This data can be used to create powerful insights that are actually usable in ads, retargeting, audience creation, and more.

You aren't just doing character development; you're building a targeted strategy to find these people and have them find you.

<u>Here's what I mean:</u>

When you go to Facebook or Google to place an ad, you'll be asked if you want to target certain people. In financial services, the only targeting option that is intuitively helpful is household income; otherwise, there's not much.

Even if I picked the top 1.00% of income earners in the U.S., it's still a market of 3 million people, not to mention one of the most expensive to show ads to. You can't help 3 million people face-to-face.

So, we need to know more, then we can narrow this down to about 100,000-250,000 with the final hero targeting resting at around 50,000-75,000 which places you perfectly to hit the 1% capture of approximately 500-750 clients.

How you accomplish this is by targeting what you know. While not exhaustive, these are some things you can target and should learn about your hero.

Targetable	Not Targetable, but useful
• Who they follow on social media • Brands they frequently use (Lux vs. Eco) • Videos on YouTube they probably watch • Websites (like blogs or news sites) they frequent • Events they attend or support • Online groups they're in • Associations/clubs they support • Preferred products (iPhone vs Android) • Activities they enjoy	• Household income growing up • Past financial traumas/setbacks • Cultural norms with money • Social influences • Beliefs about status • Other professionals they work with • Previous employers

Understand as well that all of this is evergreen strategy and not a fleeting tactic. Knowing this helps you with everything, from ads to content design, copywriting, and conversations.

Rest assured social media platforms, trends, and algorithms will change 1,000 times before your journey is complete and the work you do here will keep you and your practice adaptable.

In all of this foundational work, specificity is the key. The more you know, the more you can "triangulate" their location. This is what transforms your ideal client from the "pre-retiree engineer" into one that is 56 years old, in the top 1.00% of income earners, who frequents Kitces Blogs, YCharts, and the MotleyFool, subscribes to Kiplingers, is an iPhone user, buys Rogaine and Just For Men to preserve their youthful appearance, is a member of "Engineer Investors" Facebook group, and prefers more practical items with high quality over flashy luxury brands, so likely drives something like a Lexus LS model or an upgraded F-150 over a Maserati or BMW. If I'm looking in Texas, I'll lean toward the F-150 or perhaps a Chevy Suburban/Tahoe.

If I wanted to, I could specify that they had to have voted or support republican or democratic causes through their expressed interests. I could focus on ones with children, or even a specific company if I really wanted to focus my niche efforts through helping them better understand their benefit plans.

See what I mean?

What you tell a generic "pre-retiree engineer" could vary widely, and you'll come off as a generalist. When you get specific, you can specialize and drive the sword directly into the heart of their deepest, darkest concerns.

On your journey as the guide, it's important to understand as well why Blair Warren's *One Sentence Persuasion* course works so well.

Dreams

Think about the last time someone encouraged your dreams. For many, it's probably hard to recall. The reason I believe this is the case is because people believe that by encouraging you to chase yours, it will come at their expense. People always want you to do well, but not better than them. This is a primal human behavior driver. What if you were the person who actually did encourage their dreams? You would be almost one of a kind. The ones who need this most of all in our world, are men. For most men, when they turn 18 years old, positive affirmations stop almost entirely — it's seen as weak or too feminine. Also, it is against societal expectation for men to ask for, or seek help. If this is the case, then we most certainly are conditioned not to give it either.

Think about the young child, maybe it was you, who says "I'm going to go to Harvard and become a doctor!" only to hear from their parents and authority figures, "Maybe you should think about lots of professions and schools because, you never know, being a doctor is really hard. You should focus on a career that is sure to get you a good paying job when you graduate."

Just like that, a child's dream became 100 times harder to achieve because they were told not to believe it was possible. Because of this, they won't take risks — they were told not to by some of the most influential people in their life at the time. That's devastating!

By encouraging the dreams of adults, there's no telling the impact that you'll create to ripple through generations to come.

Failures

The biggest myth in the world today is that success, happiness, and satisfaction are all effortlessly acquired by those who are smarter than everyone or have it given to them by their parents, who were the former. The myth is that, only *some* people should have these things, when the reality is that there is enough money, resources, and happiness to go around for everyone.

People also believe that they aren't allowed to fail, and that if they do, there must be something categorically wrong with them to fail where others succeeded.

Here's the truth. There is no one who is good at anything, who was not bad at it at first. Even the prodigies who might have mastered piano at eight, sucked at it at age four — progress is relative.

There is no successful company today that did not face significant failures, setbacks, and challenges.

History has been made by people who have failed:

Thomas Edison is a prime example of perseverance. He famously failed over 1,000 times when trying to invent the light bulb. Despite these numerous setbacks, he eventually succeeded, revolutionizing the world with electric light and creating one of the most important inventions in modern history.

Walt Disney also faced significant obstacles. He was fired from a newspaper job for supposedly lacking imagination and having no good ideas. His first animation company went bankrupt, and he encountered several other business failures before finally finding success. Disney went on to create Disney Studios, now one of the largest and most successful entertainment companies globally, producing iconic characters and stories beloved worldwide.

J.K. Rowling, the author of the "Harry Potter" series, faced numerous rejections from publishers while living on welfare before her books were published. Today, she is one of the world's most successful authors, with her series selling over 500 million copies and spawning a massive franchise.

Steve Jobs experienced a major career setback when he was ousted from Apple, the company he co-founded. He also faced other business failures, such as the NeXT computer. However, Jobs returned to Apple and led it to become one of the most valuable companies in the world with revolutionary products like the iPhone, iPad, and MacBook.

Colonel Harland Sanders of Kentucky Fried Chicken (KFC) faced over 1,000 rejections when trying to sell his fried chicken recipe to restaurants. Despite these challenges, he founded KFC, which became one of the largest fast-food franchises globally.

Albert Einstein struggled academically in his early life and faced numerous rejections for his research papers and academic positions. Yet, he developed the theory of relativity and became one of the most influential physicists in history, winning the Nobel Prize.

Vincent van Gogh sold only one painting during his lifetime and was largely unrecognized as an artist, struggling with mental illness and poverty. Today, he is considered one of the greatest artists of all time, with his works valued at millions of dollars.

Henry Ford faced early business failures, including the bankruptcy of the Detroit Automobile Company. However, he revolutionized the automobile industry with the assembly line method and founded the Ford Motor Company, making cars affordable to the masses.

Oprah Winfrey faced numerous hardships, including being fired from her job as a television reporter because she was deemed "unfit for TV." She went on to become a media mogul, launching "The Oprah Winfrey Show," one of the highest-rated talk shows in television history, and built a multimedia empire.

Steven Spielberg was rejected multiple times by the University of Southern California's School of Cinematic Arts. Despite this, he became one of the most successful and influential filmmakers in history, directing blockbuster hits like "Jaws," "E.T.," "Jurassic Park," and "Schindler's List."

Just imagine what the world would be like without just these ten people referenced? The true list of this is almost limitless, but the distinction between them and others is that they persevered through failures and setbacks to achieve something great. This is why it's so important for you to understand who you might be influencing. So, justify those failures.

Tell them it's okay, it's not their fault, and they should continue, despite challenges. You're not being ruinously empathetic, you're giving them the permission that they might not be able to give themselves.

Fears

Next to misaligned relationships with money, fear is the primary driver of the problems in the world today. Money and fear together make for a very dangerous recipe and has impacted humanity since nearly the beginning of modern financial instruments and institutions.

1929: The Stock Market Crash: Rampant speculation and over-leverage created an unstable financial environment. When fear gripped investors, panic selling ensued, leading to the Great Depression. This catastrophic event wiped out millions of investors, caused massive unemployment, and led to widespread poverty and economic instability worldwide.

1970s: Stagflation Crisis: The 1970s saw a period of stagflation where high inflation combined with stagnant economic growth created a fearful environment. Governments and central banks struggled to manage the economy, leading to a loss of confidence in financial systems. The oil crises of 1973 and 1979 exacerbated the situation, causing skyrocketing energy prices and further economic turmoil. Fear of economic decline led to hoarding, increased prices, and a vicious cycle of economic stagnation.

1980s: Savings and Loan Crisis: The *Savings and Loan Crisis* of the 1980s was driven by deregulation, risky lending practices, and a lack of oversight. Misaligned relationships with money, such as the pursuit of short-term profits over long-term stability, led to widespread failures of savings and loan associations. Fear among depositors led to bank runs, further destabilizing the financial sector and necessitating a costly government bailout.

1997: Asian Financial Crisis: The *Asian Financial Crisis* in 1997 was sparked by the collapse of the Thai baht, which led to a domino effect of currency devaluations and stock market declines throughout East Asia. Misaligned relationships with money, such as excessive borrowing in foreign currencies and speculative investments, combined with fear, caused massive capital flight. Investors rapidly pulled out their funds, leading to a severe economic downturn, bankruptcies, and social unrest across the region.

2000: Dot-com Bubble Burst: The early 2000s witnessed the bursting of the dot-com bubble. Over-enthusiasm and speculative investments in internet-based companies created an unsustainable market bubble. When companies failed to deliver on high expectations, fear took hold, leading to a massive sell-off. Billions of dollars were lost, and many tech companies went bankrupt, resulting in significant job losses and economic slowdown.

2008: Global Financial Crisis: The 2008 Global Financial Crisis was one of the most severe economic downturns since the *Great Depression*. It was driven by a combination of misaligned relationships with money, such as the excessive risk-taking by banks, and fear, which caused a worldwide credit crunch. The collapse of Lehman Brothers and the subsequent panic led to a global recession, massive unemployment, and widespread foreclosures, affecting millions of lives and economies worldwide.

2010s: European Debt Crisis: The *European Debt Crisis*, beginning around 2010, saw several Eurozone countries, including Greece, Ireland, and Portugal, struggling to repay their government debt. Misaligned fiscal policies and excessive borrowing led to fear in the financial markets. Investors demanded higher yields, further increasing the cost of borrowing and leading to austerity measures, social unrest, and prolonged economic hardship in affected countries.

2020: COVID-19 Pandemic Economic Impact: The *COVID-19 Pandemic* in 2020 unleashed unprecedented global economic turmoil. Fear of the virus led to lockdowns and halted economic activities, while misaligned relationships with money, such as inadequate healthcare funding and insufficient social safety nets, exacerbated the crisis. Stock markets plummeted, unemployment soared, and governments around the world had to implement massive stimulus packages to stabilize economies.

2020s: Cryptocurrency Volatility: The rise of cryptocurrencies in the 2020s introduced a new arena of financial instability. While promising innovation, the market has been plagued by speculative investments and significant volatility. Misaligned relationships with money, such as the lure of quick profits, coupled with fear of missing out (FOMO), have led to dramatic price swings. Major crashes in the crypto market have wiped out billions of dollars, impacting investors worldwide.

Fear-based events are not going to stop anytime soon, maybe in future lifetimes, and only if we do something about it now. The truth about fear is that it's an illusion that comes into existence in order to perpetuate itself, just like cancer. Your job is to put a stop to it, not to use it to your advantage at the client's expense.

Suspicions

Few things feel as good as when you have an "I knew it" moment, even if they're followed by really bad feelings; human beings love to have their suspicions confirmed. It allows them to understand that they are not sheep, they may think for themselves, and they should not be told how to live their lives. You may think this is counter to a "good client" but it's actually exactly the client you're looking for because they are the ones who will see you as the beacon.

If your client says "I think the government did this," you can tell them that they're crazy or convince them that they're wrong, but then you'd just be like everyone and everything they already interact with. You'll be skipped for a more powerful guide who helps their clients have the "I knew it" moments. I'm not talking about confirming conspiracy theories and just agreeing with everything; it's about finding ways to be aligned.

I could say, "That's not a crazy thought, and even if the government didn't "cause" the global financial crisis in 2008, they 100% contributed to it and that is a known fact. Lax financial regulations and loose rules created conditions for nefarious characters to act, and they did. Afterwards, they even provided funding to bail these companies out of financial trouble, likely for back channel deals made without public knowledge. That statement is probably true. Do I know that for a fact? No. But the people who do know it for a fact definitely aren't going to tell us about it, so we've got to make our own moves — fair?"

That's why they're called suspicions. You can confirm them without telling your client they're right. Notice the rule here is to 'confirm their suspicions' not 'prove their suspicions to be correct'.

Throwing Rocks at Enemies

I think this is saved for last by Blair Warren, because honestly, it's the one that feels the best. Words and support are one thing, but nothing feels better than when the cavalry shows up to help take them down. During this journey, you'll identify the villains in the lives of your clients. They could be Wall Street, the IRS, an overbearing spouse, the financial system, unscrupulous insurance agents, investment managers who throw spaghetti at the wall, complacent CPAs, tax laws, etc.

The key with villains is that they create the stakes of the story — your client's story. Think about these critical stories in our history without a villain:

The American Revolution: Without the British monarchy imposing unfair taxes and laws, the colonists propose a peaceful resolution to gain more autonomy. Britain agrees, and the colonies gradually gain independence through mutual agreements and cooperation. There are no battles or revolts; instead, diplomatic talks lead to a seamless transition to independence. The colonies and Britain maintain a friendly relationship, leading to a smooth establishment of the United States.

The Civil Rights Movement: Without systemic racism and segregation laws, Martin Luther King Jr. simply requests equal rights for all citizens. The government acknowledges the oversight and promptly enacts legislation to ensure equality. The transition is smooth, with widespread public support, leading to a harmonious and inclusive society without the struggles and conflicts historically faced.

The Harry Potter Series: Without Voldemort and his Death Eaters, Harry's time at Hogwarts is filled with exploration and discovery. He excels in his studies, forms lifelong friendships, and contributes to magical research and innovation. The focus shifts to uncovering ancient magical secrets and advancing the wizarding world's knowledge. Harry and his friends lead peaceful lives, becoming respected members of the magical community.

Star Wars: Without Darth Vader and the Galactic Empire, the galaxy is a place of peace and exploration. Luke Skywalker and the Rebel Alliance focus on intergalactic diplomacy, uniting various planets and species in a grand alliance. Together, they work on solving universal challenges like space travel and planetary sustainability. The story revolves around building alliances and exploring new worlds without any significant conflicts.

The Lord of the Rings: Without Sauron, Middle-earth thrives in peace and unity. Frodo and the Fellowship embark on an epic adventure to discover and document the wonders of Middle-earth. They encounter diverse cultures, share knowledge, and build lasting bonds between different races and kingdoms. Their journey is more of an educational and cultural exchange, leading to the preservation of Middle-earth's history and beauty.

The Dark Knight Trilogy: Without villains like the Joker and Bane, Gotham City flourishes under Bruce Wayne's leadership and philanthropy. Batman's role shifts from crime-fighting to community building, focusing on education, economic development, and social programs. Gotham becomes a model city of innovation and prosperity, with Bruce Wayne leading initiatives that inspire cities worldwide.

The Terminator: Without the Terminator, Sarah Connor and her son, John, live peaceful lives. John grows up to be a leading advocate for technological ethics and artificial intelligence. Together, they spearhead movements to ensure that technology serves humanity positively. Their work leads to groundbreaking advancements in AI that benefit society, creating a safer and more ethical technological landscape.

The Hunger Games: Without President Snow and the oppressive Capitol, Panem is a unified and prosperous nation. Katniss Everdeen becomes a celebrated athlete and advocate for youth programs. She uses her platform to promote health, education, and community development. The nation thrives as districts collaborate on economic and cultural projects, ensuring a high quality of life for all citizens.

These are all great and peaceful endings, but without the villains, they hardly would have grabbed our attention for very long and they would have been very uninteresting. That's why all of the news is bad — people can't resist seeing bad news or discovering who their potential villains might be. If people didn't watch bad news, the news would be only good news, but good news (while awesome to experience personally) allows us to make lots of presumptions that terminate our attention span. You probably quit reading a lot of these long the way and just began to skim because you could guess the end.

You must be prepared to help throw rocks at their enemies. That might mean calling the mean 401(k) company operator and flexing your licenses on them to get your clients roll-over done after they got the run around.

Have you ever done this with your client? You should.

Clients are inherently anxious about calling financial institutions and don't want to do anything wrong and face potential negative outcomes because of their ignorance or oversight. Even though it seems so simple to us, it's an opportunity for you to nail this component.

I used to do this with all of my clients. I would say "Look, other than Fidelity, if you call your old company for the rollover, they're just going to try to discourage it. They'll do things like ask if you got a special and very important tax notice, if you say 'no', they'll typically say they have to mail it to you and you have to wait 30 days before completing the rollover once they send it. Here's the notice — if you don't put your money back, which we're doing, this can be treated as income for tax purposes. You have 60 days to put this money back, but we will only need the amount of time it takes them to send it to you and get it to me so that I can deposit it immediately for you. The tax notice is effectively a deterrent to rollovers, much like most of what they will say to you; they're going to send it to you anyway. There is nothing they need to know other than your desire to receive your funds via check, and they will inform you if there are additional requirements. If you want to skip all of this, I can get on the phone with you so that they don't play around and we can be done in 5 minutes. They'll ask for your permission for me to speak on your behalf and I'll take care of the rest with you on the line. If you have any objections or want to know more about anything just say so. I'm just there as your guide and advocate."

Just like that, I used a routine event as an opportunity to help throw rocks at their enemy, the 401(k) provider in this instance. Helping them alleviate the fear of being "handled" by a company that confuses them with jargon and technical and industry required information that they don't understand.

This works on other advisors too — they'll try to get territorial and say things like "I need to talk to the client" and I just say, "Nope, you don't. I'm calling you as a courtesy that you're receiving transfer documents from my client and they don't need or want you to harass them or make them feel poorly for making the decisions they feel are right for them. So, please honor the documents when they come in, and if there is anything further on behalf of the client, please feel free to send it to me. You can see that the client has confirmed because they have signed the appropriate documents, which is what is required."

You are their guide and champion. So here we go, further up the mountain.

What are their dreams?

_____

_____

_____

_____

_____

_____

_____

_____

_____

_____

_____

_____

_____

_____

_____

What are their fears? [Use tangible fears created above]

_____

_____

_____

_____

_____

_____

_____

_____

_____

_____

_____

_____

_____

_____

What are their failures?

_____

_____

_____

_____

_____

_____

_____

What are their suspicions?

_____

_____

_____

_____

_____

Who are their enemies?

_____

_____

_____

_____

_____

_____

_____

_____

_____

_____

_____

_____

_____

_____

3

BECOMING THE GUIDE

When you become the guide your clients are looking for, things start to change very quickly. To bring about this, we need to do something very important: Check our egos and humble ourselves.

If you missed the memo, the days of the lavish lifestyle, high-flying, mega-producing, 250-star diamond-platinum super advisor are over. When I think about becoming a guide in this industry, I'm reminded of this hilarious commercial I saw a few years ago.

The commercial is about a stereotypically bad financial advisor named "Dick." Throughout the ad, Dick is shown engaging in various behaviors that make him an awful advisor. He's pushy, self-centered, and clearly more interested in his own commissions than in genuinely helping his clients.

The humor in the commercial comes from exaggerated scenes where Dick gives terrible advice, disregards his clients' needs, and generally acts in a way that's completely unprofessional and unempathetic.

The overarching message is that financial advisors like Dick are out there and can cause more harm than good. The commercial suggests that viewers should be cautious of such advisors and implies that by choosing a better, more client-focused financial service, they can avoid dealing with the "Dicks" of the industry. The ad uses humor and the negative portrayal of Dick to drive home the point that people deserve better financial advice and services.

I couldn't think of a funnier commercial to do about that, so hats off to them for the creativity. More importantly, it was a big sign for me. I'm not the only one who is sick of this. For those who know me personally, I am very 'against the grain' in terms of being an advisor. I'm a former Army Infantry Squad Leader and it's about a 50/50 chance that I'm dropping an 'F Bomb' in the first meeting with complete strangers. It's not that I'm crass or uncouth, I just use that word a lot and I don't care what people think about it. You can bring elegance to the word if you try hard enough. Now, if I don't lead with authenticity, particularly for my style, I would be revealed as false at some point and then the trust in who I am is lost. By aligning to it, I not only get to be true to myself, I also help other people feel more comfortable in being themselves as well.

Turns out, some of my clients and I could write an entire book with just the 'F word', and those are the clients who moved firms with me too. Through my authenticity I become more than some monkey in a suit, pulling levers and hinging upon the market investment performance that I somehow convinced others I was responsible for, when in truth, I just made a better educated guess than they would have.

This chapter is called "Becoming the Guide" for a reason; most of people aren't one yet, just like I wasn't when I started. Most of us are still the 'hero' in our own stories, and it's true you are a hero with your own story and own journey. Many of the most impactful guides in the stories of humanity were also heroes with their own missions. If who you are is a hero, what you are is a guide, and how you serve is through the guidance provided to other heroes.

Becoming the guide your clients are seeking requires that you always abdicate the throne when they show up, and allow them to be crowned because many people still do not understand their fullest potential. Who and what they can become is so much more than they are today, and it's your role to help bring it to the surface.

If you present your hero story too strongly, they will become confused and think you are a hero like they are, on a mission, and you cannot help them.

Think about the powerful guides you know from life and popular culture.

• Gandhi	• Obi Wan	• Capt. John Miller, Saving Private Ryan
• Jesus	• Sam Wise	• Tyler Durden, Fight Club
• Mother Teresa	• Gandalf	• Tinkerbell
• Alfred from Batman	• Morpheus	• Maj. Dick Winters, Band of Brothers
• Yoda	• Jack Sparrow	• Severus Snape

All of these characters and countless more unnamed were powerful guides to the heroes of their respective plots. You also probably realize that in this light, many were heroes in their own stories, just as cool as the main character, and some were even cooler.

Becoming the guide is not about you or your qualities, as we can see, it's about how you enter someone's story, so you can both get what you want. Luckily for us, we have a framework for this but before we dive into it, we need to explore the essence of any good story if we are to tell one.

It's important that you know how wonderfully special and unique you really are, and it's equally important to know that unless you tell your story right, focusing on exactly the right aspects of you that your clients need to know, they never will.

You don't have years for people to get to know you. So, you have to address the broadest set of questions about you that will come up, so that they feel like they know you very well.

To do this, we need to activate a specific bias humans have, known as the "Halo Effect". You probably know this well, but this bias shows up when we try to understand wholly who someone is, because our brains are always in economy mode, and just make assumptions about them based on a narrow perception. If it's good, you have a halo; if not, you have horns.

This is why physically attractive people seem happier, more successful, and even more trustworthy. The truth about what makes one person more attractive comes down to the symmetry of features. That's it.

We all have our own halos but they're all different and we may not even be aware of what ours is. So, we're going to design it. Let's dive in.

The first thing to do, as it relates to the hero you seek to guide, is crafting a powerful backstory. Your backstory should have two components. It should explain your origins and include struggles and triumphs that ultimately led to your epiphany that brought you to the place of empathy and authority you stand in today. Once you've hooked them with your story, they need to know what your core values and beliefs are; they need to know what guides you. If you haven't already, take the time to define some core values and beliefs others can get behind. Pick 5 values — things like integrity, candor, curiosity, family, independence — and 3 principles to live by, like "Bad news doesn't get better with time", "Never ask you to do anything I would not be willing to do myself", or "Do unto others as you would yourself", etc.

Most importantly, be sure you know why it matters. The character you are for clients should offer a unique perspective or point of view. You should offer a distinct viewpoint about finances, planning, insurance, or investing.

Your fresh insights offer a distinct and unique path to their desired transformation, not reiterating the same things everyone hears constantly.

It's very possible to make your character so attractive that it's not relatable or believable, so you need to build in personal flaws and vulnerabilities that add the essential humanizing elements you need to connect your audience to your characters.

You should also be able to demonstrate areas of growth; this allows you to show self-awareness.

Enhance your charisma. It's worth noting here that for a typical advisor, this may be difficult to do. So much of our profession requires pragmatism, logic, and a balanced demeanor, but if you can step out here, you'll stand out.

The way to understand this is by understanding that you are transforming too and that transformation is from financial advisor to a financial thought leader.

Most of your charisma will come from your communication style, and what I'll say to you is that you will attract vastly superior and meaningful relationships using the opposite communication style from what you are accustomed to.

The best and fastest way to develop your style is to get clear on your message. There's a book called StorySelling that can provide a powerful framework for how you tell your stories. Before you improve your style, be sure you can tell your whole story, end to end. Just honor the idea here that the more you sound and tell stories like every advisor, the more you'll be one.

As you continue to refine all of this, make no mistake — you are doing the most impactful work for yourself possible. Here's a comprehensive framework to guide you:

Relatable Backstory

Start with your origins, detailing where you came from, your initial motivations, and the early challenges you faced. Highlight key struggles and the triumphs that followed. Finally, share your epiphany—the moment when everything changed for you. This backstory creates a relatable and human foundation for your journey.

Exercise: Reflect on Your Backstory. Spend a few minutes writing about your origins. Include where you grew up, key influences in your early life, and significant events that shaped you. Consider the following:

- What were your biggest struggles early on?
- What triumphs did you experience?
- What was your epiphany moment?

_____

_____

_____

_____

_____

_____

_____

_____

_____

_____

_____

_____

_____

_____

Core Values and Principles

Identify Your Core Values and Principles Sit in a quiet space and reflect on moments in your life that felt deeply fulfilling or meaningful. Write down these moments and then identify what value or principle was at play. Aim to identify at least five core values. Consider these prompts:

- When did you feel most proud of yourself?

- What achievements have brought you the most satisfaction?

- In moments of conflict, what principles guided your actions?

_____

_____

Unique POV

Define your unique Point of View. How do you see things differently from others in your field? What unique insights or perspectives do you bring to the table? This POV will set you apart and attract those who resonate with your vision.

Exercise: Take a few minutes to brainstorm what sets you apart from others in your field. Write down any unique insights, perspectives, or approaches you have. Reflect on these questions:

- How do you see your industry differently?
- What unique solutions do you offer?

_____

_____

_____

_____

_____

_____

_____

_____

_____

_____

_____

_____

_____

_____

_____

Personal Flaws and Vulnerabilities

Acknowledge your personal flaws and vulnerabilities. Choose three non-detrimental flaws that humanize you, such as being a perfectionist, overly cautious, or sometimes procrastinating. Additionally, identify two areas of growth where you are actively working to improve. This honesty builds trust and relatability.

Exercise: List three non-detrimental personal flaws and two areas where you are actively seeking growth. Be honest and introspective. Consider:

- What personal traits do you struggle with?
- What steps are you taking to improve in certain areas?

_____

_____

_____

_____

_____

_____

_____

_____

_____

_____

_____

_____

_____

_____

Charisma

Develop your storytelling charisma. How should you tell
your story to captivate your audience? Use humor, vivid
imagery, and relatable anecdotes to make your content more

engaging. Consider different formats, such as videos, podcasts, or written blogs, to connect with your audience on various levels.

Exercise: Write a short story or anecdote that showcases your personality. Practice telling it in different formats (written, video, podcast). Think about:

- How can you make your story more engaging?
- What elements of humor or vivid imagery can you add?

_____

_____

_____

_____

_____

_____

_____

_____

_____

_____

_____

_____

_____

_____

Relatable Aspirations

Identify three aspirational goals that you share with your hero. These can be philosophical and deeply personal, like striving for financial freedom, building a legacy, or achieving personal fulfillment. Shared dreams create deep bonds and inspire your audience to join you on your journey.

Exercise: Write down three aspirational goals that you share with your target audience. Make sure they are philosophical and deeply meaningful. Reflect on:

- What dreams do you have that align with your audience's goals?

- How can you inspire your audience to pursue these aspirations?

_____

_____

_____

_____

_____

_____

_____

_____

_____

_____

_____

_____

_____

_____

_____

Storytelling Ability

Master your "why." Clearly articulate why you do what you do. This involves sharing your deeper motivations and the change you hope to bring about. Your "why" should resonate with your audience and inspire them to take action. *It's important that your story has an arc — a beginning, middle, and end.*

Exercise: Write a paragraph explaining why you do what you do. Make it personal and passionate. Ask yourself:

- What motivates you every day?
- What change do you hope to bring about?

_____

_____

_____

_____

_____

_____

_____

_____

_____

_____

_____

_____

_____

_____

Authority

Establish your authority. What credentials, experience, or expertise do you have that qualify you to guide others? This could include professional certifications, years of experience, or notable achievements in your field. Your authority reassures your audience that they are in capable hands.

Exercise: Craft a concise statement that highlights your authority. If you don't have any yet, it's okay. Reflect on:

- What qualifications do you have?
- What have you experienced that enabled you to learn what you know?
- What hardship have you endured to earn the right to tell the tale?
- How do these credentials build trust with your audience?

_____

_____

_____

_____

_____

_____

_____

_____

_____

_____

_____

_____

_____

_____

Consistency and Reliability

Build your movement with consistency and reliability. Choose one primary platform where you will consistently share your message and engage with your audience. Master this platform before expanding to others, ensuring that your presence is strong and dependable.

Exercise: Choose one primary platform (e.g., blog, social media, YouTube) to focus on initially. Create a content calendar for the next month. Consider:

- How often will you post?
- What type of content will you share?

_____

_____

_____

_____

_____

_____

_____

_____

_____

_____

_____

_____

_____

Transformational Impact

Showcase your value through client success stories. Craft three detailed examples of clients who have experienced significant positive change due to your guidance. These stories should illustrate the transformational impact you can have, providing tangible evidence of your effectiveness.

Write three detailed client success stories. Focus on the transformation they experienced with your help. Think about:

- What challenges did the client face and what emotions were they grappled by?
- How did you help them overcome these challenges in more than just a financial way?

Story 1:

_____

_____

_____

_____

_____

_____

_____

_____

_____

_____

_____

_____

_____

_____

_____

Story 2:

_____

_____

_____

_____

_____

_____

_____

_____

_____

_____

_____

_____

_____

_____

Story 3:

_____

_____

_____

_____

_____

_____

_____

_____

_____

_____

_____

_____

_____

_____

_____

Engagement

Foster a sense of community and belonging. Think about how you can create a supportive and interactive environment for your audience. This could involve hosting webinars, creating a private online group, or organizing in-person events. Engagement builds loyalty and a sense of shared purpose.

Plan an engagement strategy, such as starting an online community or hosting a webinar. Outline the steps and resources needed. Consider:

- How will you interact with your audience

- In what areas are you best equipped or knowledgeable?

_____

_____

_____

_____

_____

_____

_____

_____

_____

_____

_____

_____

_____

- What activities or events will you organize
- How will you build momentum?

_____

_____

_____

_____

_____

_____

_____

_____

_____

_____

_____

_____

_____

_____

_____

Mission and Vision

Clarify your mission and vision. What intrinsically drives you? What long-term change do you hope to bring about in your field or in the lives of your clients? Your mission and vision should be inspiring and clearly communicated, serving as a guiding light for your journey.

Mission and vision statements are different. A mission can change; a vision does not. Your mission might be to provide the best in class financial services for your niche, but your vision should be a world where your niche doesn't have to deal with the problems anymore — forever.

Write a mission statement and a vision statement. Make sure they are clear, inspiring, and aligned with your core values. Reflect on:

- What is your ultimate goal?
- What change do you want to see in the world?

Mission (what mission you're on for now)

_____

_____

_____

_____

_____

_____

_____

_____

_____

_____

_____

_____

_____

_____

_____

Vision (what mission you're on forever). This *should not* change, but can, as much as you need it to until you're sure it's the best fit for you.

_____

_____

_____

_____

_____

_____

_____

_____

_____

_____

_____

_____

_____

_____

_____

As you're learning, each section you complete helps you complete the next one. So, be sure to do the work as you go along, even if it sucks or you can't think about it properly right now. The point of these exercises is to create a tangible foundation to build on; you will do lots of refinement to these as you continue on your path to transformation. In the last section I'll show you how to bring everything to life effortlessly.

DESIGN YOUR JOURNEY

All stories are built the same way. Fair warning — you might become that person who figures out the end of the movie within the first 10 minutes to the dismay of those around you, but it's a critical understanding to have.

Many authors have fine works on this, but here's the gist — stories are the most captivating tool to ever exist; they've worked since the dawn of time to capture our imagination, for hours at a time. Nothing else does this. Nothing!

It's because they (the good ones people actually listen to) follow a very specific set of instructions with a specific structure. That's the reason nearly 100% of movies are made this way. In fact, they have a specific event every year to allow and award movies that do not follow this structure — The SunDance Film Festival.

So, we need a structure, but what kind? A man named Donald Miller has already blazed this trail for us with his StoryBrand, or SB7 framework. Don't worry, you won't need the book for this, but to truly master your heroes' journey, I would highly recommend it.

What his philosophy focuses on is removing confusion from your offer by translating it into a story. To do this, he decanted several books and transformed them into his framework. This framework has been adapted several times by marketers like ClickFunnels Russell Brunson, Neil Patel, Sabri Suby, and more.

Now, let's understand marketing as an industry for a moment, most marketers today, myself included are not very inventive. This is mostly because marketers didn't invent humans either, and that is the primary target of marketing.

Knowing this, we can appreciate that marketers are like chefs; your ecosystem is the recipe. Just like you can innovate a dish and call it yours, the same goes for marketing. So, when we discover a framework that does the trick, we are honoring one of the fundamental components of effective marketing.

Never do research twice. They say you can tell who the pioneers are from all of the arrows in their back, and this is no different. We want to become the Steve Jobs of marketing as much as we want to become Jack Sparrow or Captain

BlackBeard. You'll need the work you did in the previous chapter here, so go back and complete it if you haven't already.

Exercise: Crafting Your Client's Journey with the SB7 Framework

Part 1: Identify the Hero

- ○ Who are your clients? Describe their demographic (age, gender, occupation) and psychographic characteristics (values, interests, lifestyle).

- ○ What are their primary goals and aspirations? What do they truly desire?

_____

_____

_____

_____

_____

_____

_____

_____

_____

_____

_____

_____

_____

_____

_____

Example: My clients are middle-aged professionals seeking financial stability and growth. They value security, trust, and personalized advice.

Part 2: Understand the Problem

- **External Problems:** What tangible issues do your clients face?

- **Internal Problems:** How do these external issues make your clients feel?

- **Philosophical Problems:** What larger, universal challenge does this problem connect to?

- **Villains:** Who or what are the antagonistic forces in their lives?

_____

_____

_____

_____

_____

_____

_____

_____

_____

_____

_____

_____

_____

Example: External: Confusing investment options. Internal: Anxiety about financial future. Philosophical: Everyone deserves financial security. Villain: Misleading financial advice.

Part 3: Position Yourself as the Guide

- How do you show empathy for your clients' struggles?

- What credentials, experience, or success stories establish your authority?

_____

_____

_____

_____

_____

_____

_____

_____

_____

_____

_____

_____

_____

Example: I empathize by sharing my own financial challenges and how I overcame them. My authority is established through 20 years of experience and numerous client success stories.

Part 4: Create a Clear Plan

- **Process:** What is the step-by-step process you will guide your clients through?

- **Agreement:** What will you do, and what do you expect from your clients?

_____

_____

_____

_____

_____

_____

_____

_____

_____

_____

_____

_____

_____

_____

Example: Process: 1. Initial consultation 2. Personalized financial plan 3. Regular review sessions. Agreement: I provide expert advice; you implement the recommendations.

Part 5: Call Them to Action

- **Direct Calls to Action:** What explicit steps should they take now?

- **Transitional Calls to Action:** What low-risk actions can help build the relationship?

Example: Direct: Schedule a free consultation. Transitional: Download my free financial planning guide.

Part 6: Envision the Result

- What positive outcomes will your clients achieve by following your plan?

- What failures or negative outcomes will they avoid?

_____

_____

_____

_____

_____

_____

_____

_____

_____

_____

_____

_____

Example: Success: Achieve financial stability and growth. Avoid: Financial mismanagement and anxiety about the future.

Part 7: Illustrate the Transformation

- Describe how your clients will transform from their current state (X) to their desired state (Y).

Example: Transform from feeling overwhelmed and anxious to being confident and secure in their financial future.

Putting It All Together:

Use the insights from each part to craft a narrative for your client's journey. Here's a template to help you combine the elements:

Framework:

Meet [Hero's Name], a [Hero's Demographic and Psychographic Details] who dreams of [Hero's Primary Goal]. However, they face [External Problem], which makes them feel [Internal Problem]. They believe that [Philosophical Problem] shouldn't exist. In their life, [Villain] is the antagonistic force.

But then, they meet [You], who understands their struggles because [Empathy Statement]. With [Credentials and Authority], [Your Name] is the perfect guide to help them.

[You] offer a clear plan: [Process Steps]. Together, they agree that [Your Role] and [Client's Role].

To take the first step, [Hero's Name] needs to [Direct Call to Action]. As a low-risk start, they can [Transitional Call to Action].

By following this plan, [Hero's Name] will achieve [Positive Outcomes] and avoid [Negative Outcomes].

Ultimately, [Hero's Name] transforms from [Current State] to [Desired State], feeling [Positive Emotional Outcome].

Example:

Meet John, a middle-aged professional seeking financial stability and growth who dreams of achieving financial freedom and security for his family. However, he faces confusing investment options, which makes him feel anxious and overwhelmed about his financial future. He believes that financial instability shouldn't exist. In his life, misleading financial advice is the antagonistic force.

But then, he meets you, who understands his struggles because you've faced similar financial challenges and overcame them. With 20 years of experience and numerous client success stories, you are the perfect guide to help him.

You offer a clear plan: 1. Initial consultation, 2. Personalized financial plan, 3. Regular review sessions. Together, they agree that you will provide expert advice and John will implement the recommendations.

To take the first step, John needs to schedule a free consultation. As a low-risk start, he can download your free financial planning guide.

By following this plan, John will achieve financial stability and growth and avoid financial mismanagement and anxiety.

Ultimately, John transforms from feeling overwhelmed and anxious to being confident, secure in his financial future, relieved, and empowered.

Once you're done with this, turn it into the story you tell when asked – what do you do?

Framework:

"Many people are trying to ___ so that they can ___, but they typically struggle with [Part II]. I feel this deeply because ___, which is why I ___, when I guide people on this path, we follow ___ and agree to ___, typically starting with ___. What usually happens is they ___ while also avoiding ___, allowing them to really transform themselves from ___ to ___."

Example:

"Many people are trying to achieve financial freedom so that they can provide security for their families, but they typically struggle with confusing investment options and misleading financial advice. I feel this deeply because I've faced similar financial challenges and overcame them, which is why I've dedicated my career to helping others navigate these waters. When I guide people on this path, we follow a clear plan: we start with an initial consultation, then develop a personalized financial plan, and have regular review sessions to stay on track. We agree that I provide expert advice and they implement the recommendations, typically starting with a free consultation to get things rolling. What usually happens is they achieve financial stability and growth while also avoiding financial mismanagement and anxiety, allowing them to really transform themselves from feeling overwhelmed and anxious to being confident and secure in their financial future."

Now we're niching. I'm often asked if this will repel clients that would otherwise be a fit. The answer is really in the question.

Otherwise be a fit for what? Paying you?

You can't get serious about your business if you're just trying to make money. Besides, if you take a client that isn't a fit for you, you're taking them off their search unnecessarily and preventing them from their transformation.

It's your business, and your long-term success is the best thing to ensure so you can stay on your path. If you're just starting out, take care of business but come up with a plan for exclusive focus as soon as you possibly can.

5

THE ATOMIC OFFER

No matter your thoughts or opinions about the use of the atomic or thermonuclear weapons, we can't deny their sheer power and "table turning" abilities. Your offer should be the same. No matter how "small" you think you are, when equipped with an atomic offer, even the "biggest" players will stop and listen when you speak.

If this is difficult to imagine, apply it to real life. The countries of Taiwan and China have been in a territorial conflict for as long as I can remember. Every year, Taiwan says they're sovereign, China disagrees and a myriad of military exercises and drills ensue to posture their way into another stalemate — just to repeat the following year.

But what if Taiwan had nuclear weapons too? Sure, we could speculate about escalations but the reality is that China would do a lot less peacocking and Taiwan would be able to stand on their own two feet.

So, regardless of the size of your business or how long you've been in the game, get ready to leave all that behind. In this chapter, you'll learn how to transform your standard offerings into an atomic offer that's impossible to resist.

Slightly Lethal Payload?

That's what 99% of financial advisors bring into the battlefield every single day.

Here's what it typically looks like:

- **You have a process** between 4-6 steps, likely adapted from the CFP body of knowledge, and depicted as a circular or infinite cycle.

- **You have a value proposition** that's mostly about you, mentioning how you're different and sprinkling in some buzzwords about understanding clients' needs or being people-centric.

- **You have a "needs-based" approach** where you offer consultations for free, hoping to find a problem to solve without presenting any real solutions upfront.

- **You get paid after all the work is done,** often leaving you chasing payments and having to justify your value afterward.

- **You talk about dozens of financial topics,** hoping to find something that sparks further conversation, often leaving clients overwhelmed.

- **Your investment management pitch** involves discussing asset allocation and rates of return, which sounds similar to every other advisor out there.

- **You constantly combat external noise** from influencers like Dave Ramsay or Jim Cramer, who often undermine your strategies.

- **You repeatedly reconvince clients** to stick with their strategies, battling their doubts and market anxieties.

Sound familiar? It's only slightly lethal because it will only work on people who aren't paying attention. But let's go a little further just to be sure.

You package all of this up by navigating revisions and removing certain words some compliance analyst red-lined just to feel like they did something, and you get approval for your event, talk, or webinar a week after you needed it... and your thing is in 3 days.

Despite the frustration, you press on, knowing that even though you feel cringy and salesy — this is the way. "That's what I did," your manager or leader will say. "Just do this for a few years and everything changes," says the veteran advisor in passing.

Don't worry, you aren't alone; I did this too when I started in financial services. I started as the one that forces you to go house-to-house, knocking on doors, trying to find people with old rollovers that are just small enough to get the maximum A share, upfront sales commission on.

During the summer of 2016, I walked over 400 miles tallying up nearly 5,000 doors that I knocked on. In the end, I had to get their information to call and have something to offer when I did — for me, it was a webinar. I never did any events but I did get over 800 phone numbers, and from that, created about 100 new households in 12 months.

This took forever and while the dinosaurs were right, it did work — I was door knocking from 7am to 12pm, meeting clients from 1pm to 5pm, and door knocking from 6pm to 8pm for 5 to 6 days per week. That didn't include all the time I spent writing 'thank you' cards, following up, driving to people's houses and more.

So, yes, let's set the level that if you throw enough spaghetti on the wall, something will stick.

Around the same time I started in financial services, a man named Rusell Brunson was setting the world record for the most money made selling from stage in 90 minutes — $3.2 million dollars.

What? $3.2 million dollars in 90 minutes? Yes.

What could possibly be more powerful than all my hard work and determination?

It was how he increased the perceived value of his offer that did this for him. In doing the same thing as Russell, we can make our offers atomic as well.

Before we dive into atomic offer creation, let's explore in a totally different industry how this works using something that you personally can relate to:

Let's use pet care in this example, if you have any, and ever board them before you travel anywhere — you understand what a racket this is. We have two Iggys (Italian Greyhounds), and anytime we travel anywhere, we take them to their day care at a whopping $100 per day. I could take them to any doggie day care and it would be about the same cost.

We chose this commodity provider over others not based on reviews, or testimonials but because of their offer. Their website wasn't the best one, but what they had to offer was unrivaled.

When you make an atomic offer, you'll see quickly why everything else you've held on a pedestal doesn't always work, like reviews and testimonials.

People trust others' opinions for products, sure, but no one knows what they want or need more than ourselves. When your offer becomes atomic, what your website looks like, what your slide deck looks like, or your business card won't matter anymore.

Let's compare a slightly lethal offer with an atomic one using a doggy daycare as an example, then we'll explore how to apply this to our world.

Slightly Lethal Offer – Doggy Day Care:

"The best place to take your dog!" – $50 / pet / day

- Individual sleeping areas for your pups
- Lots of fun social interaction
- 24/7 camera monitoring
- Climate-controlled facility
- Fun events
- Dogs love us!

Atomic Offer – Doggy Day Care:

"The doggy staycation, so good that they won't want to leave once you're back!" – $80 / pet / day

- **Luxury Sleep Pods**: Let your pups bask in luxury with individual sleep pods – plus, get live updates while they snooze!

- **Epic Playtime**: Enjoy your travels with peace of mind knowing your "baby" is having the time of their life with bubble, splash, and playtime 7 times a day!

- **Total Transparency**: Be confident in your pup's care and safety with transparent 24/7 facility monitoring through our easy-to-use app!

- **Perfect Climate**: Sleep better knowing your pup experiences a cool, consistent 69 degrees both day and night!

- **Custom Itineraries**: Curate their experience upon check-in with a customizable itinerary that keeps them engaged the entire time – they'll hardly know you're gone!

- **Happy Homecoming**: Finally, come home to a dog that isn't crying and traumatized from your absence!

Plus!

- **Precise Care**: Feed and sleep times followed exactly as per your instructions – no exceptions!

- **Spa Treatment**: Stays over 3 days include a luxurious bath and nail trim – because your pup deserves the best!

- **Home Comforts**: Bring their security blanket and favorite toy to keep them comfy and happy.

- **Movie Nights**: Pet movie night, every night, your pup can enjoy their favorite flicks!

- **Story Time**: Optional story time sessions to lull your pup into sweet dreams.

So, where do your pups go? The second offer is more expensive and the website isn't as pretty, but does that matter? Not for me as their ideal customer — a person who loves their pets; not so much that I need to take them everywhere, but enough to not want them to stay in the equivalent of a shelter just to save some money.

You'll figure some people don't want that and it could deter potential clients or customers, and you'd be right — that's the point.

Dog house #1 can't have 1,000 pets at once; your business would collapse if you had that many households to serve, tomorrow.

To design your offer correctly, do some backwards planning. In other words, begin with the end in mind.

For most, your future income will come from financial planning fees, insurance commission and renewals, upfront annuity sales, and ongoing investment management wrap fees. So, decide right now, how much is enough?

It might seem like "never", but trust me, you will arrive at a place where more money doesn't equal more satisfaction, and the last thing you want to do is become so good at trading time and stress for money that you don't know how to stop.

Let's say it's $500,000 per year, and we'll just use investments for this, everyone is different and you're a financial advisor — crunch the numbers for yourself.

To make $500,000 a year on a 50% pay out, you would need to manage $100 million at a rate of 1.00%, more if your platform auto calculates breakpoints.

You can't manage 1,000 households with $100,000 AUM each. But you could definitely manage 100 households with $1M AUM each. Giving yourself 5 years to do this, you'll need to find one to two ideal clients per month on average, and assume it will even out at the end.

Now, I know how to build my offer, everything is focused on the $1M client as it relates to investing. Despite being a full service planner, I'm leaning in with this offer to attract people from shark infested waters over to my oasis meant just for them:

Here's the competition SLO a.k.a. "Dick's Offer":

- Low fees
- Quality investments
- Custom solutions
- Direct manager access
- Quarterly net updates
- Hedging and alternatives
- SMA/UMA
- Tax harvesting
- Covered options

The list is not exhaustive but here are some firms with this exact offer:

- Fidelity
- Vanguard
- Fisher Investments
- Edward Jones Investments
- Morgan Stanely
- Merril Lynch
- Charles Schwab
- Ameriprise

- LPL Financial
- Raymond James

Sorry… nevermind! It is exhaustive; that's everyone. But let's check mutuals too.

- New York Life
- Mass Mutual
- Northwestern Mutual

Yep, it's them too, but theirs is even worse.

Here's an atomic version of this (steal it if you want to, I can do this all day)

"Turn your collections of good investments into a supercharged strategy."

- Size matters, which is why you shouldn't be paying the same fees as investors with smaller accounts. Your costs are always customized to reflect your achievements as you build your wealth with us.

- Ditch the cookie cutter, everyone has access to the same stock market returns but not all experiences are equal. We'll help you concentrate your strategy, so that your portfolio can be a reflection of your beliefs and values while working towards your goals.

- Choose confidently, knowing all of our solutions have been deeply vetted by our investment team to help ensure quality, consistency, and reliability — no penny stocks or speculation.

- Get in on the ground floor with exclusive access to your PM team directly to help keep you involved, informed, and engaged with your strategy.

- Stay up-to-date, even when you're too busy, with quarterly communications and webinars from our investment team that cut through the jargon and fluff so you can skip trying to decide everything and just get the facts in a way that makes sense to you.

- Forget buy and hold blues and emotional rollercoasters by bolstering your strategy, with design and alternative investing strategies including structured notes and private placements.

- Clear the runway for your strategy with hyper focused strategies from factors, to sectors, SMAs, UMAs, and even building your own mutual fund, known as "direct indexing".

- Get help keeping the ongoing tax burden in your portfolio down with thoughtful tax loss harvesting that zeroes in on your capital gains budget to help maintain a growth focus of your strategy, helping you to avoid surprise tax bills every year.

- Move down your investing adventure with a strategy that involves you as much or as little as you want, reflects who you are, is easily understood and communicated — all while following proven strategies and using established processes, so you don't have to risk it all on outdated strategies like options trading or get taken to the cleaners with cryptocurrency.

Are you getting this?

I am still offering the same product or service, but how they experience it is what's different.

What you've seen so far is the main difference of the work you're doing, you're taking something that is a feature and representing it as a massive benefit using things that resonate deeply with your audience.

Everything, everything, everything you say or show your clients should go through this process.

Doing this can seem daunting but it's actually quite simple with a framework and it involves 3 steps. You'll eventually do this for every offer you have, but just work on nailing one before moving on.

Step 1: Break out your service

In this step, your job here is to think of every single thing you could do for your clients to basically guarantee that they will be successful. You won't use these words obviously, but by the end they will feel this way.

So, what could you give or do for them? Write down everything, even if there's no way you would or even could. The point is to get all the surface level ideas out of the way, so the good ones can come.

Here are some examples to start:

- Fly to each client's house and place trades in their home
- Take them to your beach house for a weekend
- Be available 24/7, 365 for phone calls
- Explain the strategy to every family member
- Give them a daily portfolio update

These are ridiculous, but even if it would never work, put it down — you'll see why.

_____

_____

_____

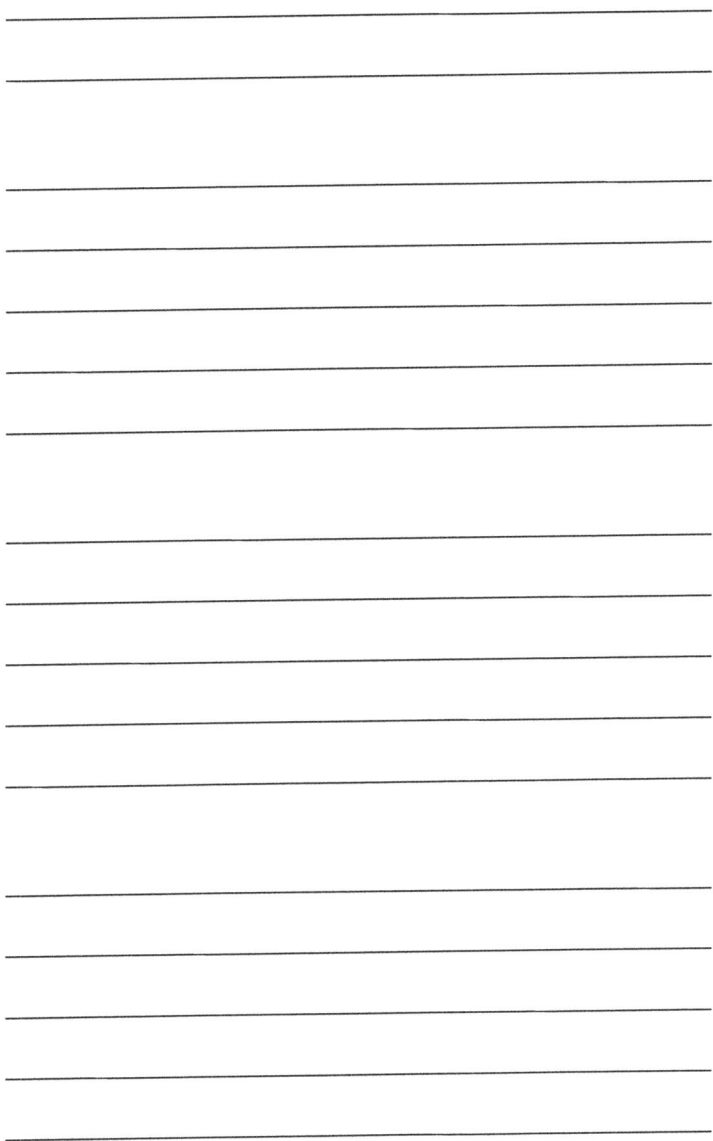

_____

_____

_____

_____

_____

_____

_____

_____

_____

Step 2: Break out your product / service offer

It's important to know that how and who you are is your service, or how you serve, then your process and your deliverables are your product and this is a little more tangible to do.

Extra bonus points if you give this offer framework a name like "Platinum Planning" or something.

If your process has steps, this is where to start. Think about each step, each meeting. Write them down, on the first line and with the lines underneath it, list out all of the things they "get" from that meeting, even if it's an intangible understanding.

You must understand that as comfortable as you are with financial services, most people have no clue what to expect and probably have some apprehension to agreeing to anything they can't see the end of.

Step One:

_____

_____

_____

_____

_____

_____

_____

_____

_____

_____

_____

_____

Step Two:

_____

_____

_____

_____

_____

_____

_____

_____

_____

_____

_____

_____

_____

_____

Step Three:

_____

_____

_____

_____

_____

_____

_____

_____

_____

_____

_____

Step Four:

_____

_____

_____

_____

_____

_____

_____

_____

_____

_____

_____

_____

_____

_____

Step Five:

_____

_____

_____

_____

_____

_____

_____

_____

_____

_____

_____

_____

_____

_____

_____

Be sure, under each of your steps, to write down everything you do or show on that step.

Here's an example of what step one could look like:

Step One: Initial Consultation / Discovery Meeting

What They Get:

- **Net Worth Assessment:** A detailed and precise calculation of your current financial standing.

- **Financial Health Check:** A comprehensive analysis of your financial health, tailored to your specific needs.

- **3 Pitfalls to Avoid:** Key financial traps you should steer clear of to protect your assets.

- **3 Opportunities to Capture:** Exciting opportunities identified to boost your financial growth.

- **Game-Changer Insight:** One crucial strategy or piece of advice that could significantly impact your financial future.

- **Retirement Readiness Assessment:** An evaluation of your current retirement plan and what adjustments can maximize your future security.

- **Debt Management Review:** An assessment of your current debts with strategies to reduce and manage them effectively.

- **Tax Efficiency Check:** Personalized advice on how to optimize your tax situation and keep more of your hard-earned money.

- **Investment Portfolio Review:** An in-depth look at your current investments with suggestions for diversification and growth.

- **Insurance Coverage Assessment:** Ensuring you have the right insurance coverage to protect against unforeseen events.

- **Estate Planning Overview:** Basic guidance on setting up a will, trusts, and other estate planning tools to ensure your legacy is preserved.

- **Cash Flow Analysis:** Insights into your income and expenses, identifying ways to improve your cash flow and save more.

- **Financial Goal Setting:** Helping you articulate and prioritize your short-term and long-term financial goals.

You can decide on what and how much of these things to offer or add, depending on your practice, but this is the essence of offer building and you'll apply this to every phase of the journey you take people on. In many ways, you're also gamifying this journey for people so they understand the bigger milestones and smaller checkpoints along the way. You're creating something irresistible and highly accessible.

Step 3: Rebuild into atomic offer

Now let's activate it. To do this, we can use the framework above but we're going to really drive into what we understand about our ideal clients. For this example, we're creating an offer for our "pre-retiree engineer" that we elevated and supercharged in the beginning.

Step One: Initial Consultation / Discovery Meeting

What They Get:

- **Net Worth Assessment:** Gain a precise and detailed understanding of your financial standing. We'll provide a thorough analysis that complements your existing spreadsheets, ensuring nothing is overlooked. *So, you can feel confident about your financial position and avoid any surprises down the road.*

- **Financial Health Check:** A comprehensive review of your entire financial situation, verifying your calculations and highlighting any potential blind spots you might have missed. *So, you can be assured everything is on track and avoid potential pitfalls that could disrupt your plans.*

- **3 Pitfalls to Avoid:** Identify common retirement pitfalls that even the most meticulous planners can overlook, and learn strategies to avoid them, safeguarding your savings. *So, you can protect your hard-earned money and avoid costly mistakes.*

- **3 Opportunities to Capture:** Uncover specific opportunities tailored to your unique situation that can enhance your retirement portfolio and secure your financial future. *So, you can maximize your returns and avoid missing out on valuable opportunities.*

- **Game-Changer Insight:** Receive targeted advice that could significantly optimize your current financial strategies, offering new perspectives that align with your analytical mindset. *So, you can fine-tune your approach and avoid stagnation in your financial growth.*

- **Retirement Readiness Assessment:** Evaluate whether your current retirement plan will provide the security and comfort you desire. We'll run the numbers and suggest adjustments to ensure you're on track. *So, you can retire with peace of mind and avoid any shortfalls in your retirement income.*

- **Debt Management Review:** Analyze your current debts with a focus on optimizing repayment strategies, helping you to manage or eliminate debt efficiently before retirement. *So, you can be debt-free sooner and avoid the stress of lingering debt.*

- **Tax Efficiency Check:** Explore tax optimization techniques to ensure you're maximizing your retirement income while minimizing your tax liabilities, using data-driven strategies. *So, you can* keep more of your money and avoid paying unnecessary taxes.

- **Investment Portfolio Review:** A detailed review of your investments to ensure they align with your retirement goals and risk tolerance. We'll provide data-backed suggestions for improvement. *So, you can grow your wealth confidently and avoid high-risk investments that don't fit your profile.*

- **Insurance Coverage Assessment:** Confirm that you have the right insurance coverage to protect yourself and your loved ones from unforeseen events, with a detailed risk analysis. *So, you can safeguard your family's future and avoid gaps in your coverage.*

- **Estate Planning Overview:** Guidance on setting up a will, trusts, and other estate planning tools to preserve your legacy. We'll explain the details clearly and answer any questions you have. *So, you can ensure your wishes are honored and avoid legal complications for your heirs.*

- **Cash Flow Analysis:** A thorough examination of your income and expenses to find ways to improve your cash flow, ensuring you can maintain your lifestyle comfortably in retirement. *So, you can enjoy your retirement without financial worry and avoid running out of money.*

- **Financial Goal Setting:** Help you articulate and prioritize your retirement goals, setting a clear and actionable path to achieve them. We'll create a roadmap that's easy to follow and adjust as needed. *So, you can achieve your dreams and avoid drifting without a clear plan.*

As much as I want to say this ought to and should fly through compliance easily, you can imagine a compliance officer reading anything an advisor creates and just saying, "Yep, looks good!" Compliance professionals are important members of our community and help protect people, and most importantly, their employers. So just understand that, they're de-risking your content, so they're comfortable with it.

Take revisions and changes in stride; you've got too much to do. I've deleted entire sections of webinars, offers, and presentations, instead of revising them, for the sake of speed. It doesn't matter that much because anything I feel that I left out, I can address in person, and even if compliance analysts chop your stuff up considerably, you can always find a broker-dealer that is more lenient on the compliance piece to hang your hat. But even if you don't, your content will still be considerably more effective than most advisor content.

Now that you've dialed your offer in and truly made it amazing, we need to make your offer available to those who aren't ready yet by showing them the path. This is your **Value Ascent:** the journey you take people on from start to finish.

This is what we'll do next.

6

THE VALUE ASCENT

One of the concepts that has absolutely revolutionized the way I go to market today is the value ascent. When you ascend your prospective clients in the right way, you create a stream of business that is hard to turn off. So much so that even after transitioning full time from financial services to financial advisor marketing, I frequently get messages and emails inquiring whether I am taking on new clients. Depending on the client, I sometimes take them into my private practice that I maintain for certain cases, or otherwise, refer them to trusted and vetted advisors at my firm.

I learned this lesson from painstakingly trying to get over 3,000 people on my email list to the same monthly webinar focused on tax strategies for an entire year. What's strange is that, it was almost always the same people who attended the same webinar over and over, hoping that there would be new information, but there never was. "That's the point of webinars right?" I responded to my partner who was concerned about diminishing attendance at our regularly scheduled webinars.

"What do you mean?" he replied.

"Well, you just do the webinar over and over until no one comes to it anymore and then you make a new one." I confidently rebutted to him.

We continued on like this for months until I started looking at the data behind our email campaigns inviting people to our webinars.

It got a lot of clicks, engagement, and interaction from unique sources, but the only ones who showed up were the same people. It started with only 5-7, and built up to a regularly recurring audience of 20-30 people. Mind you, these were business owners. So, as a financial advisor, I thought we were doing pretty good.

"Why aren't these people converting?" I thought to myself as I scratched my head, wondering what I was doing wrong. I knew there had to be something that I was missing. Fortunately for me, I was about to get a big leg up as a marketer and I attended Russell Brunson's "Funnel Hacking Live Event" virtually. This event is a culmination of all of the most successful funnel marketers on earth, trying to steal each other's ideas and win the prizes and accolades in the following year. I loved it because I didn't really have any ideas at the time; I just got to steal everyone else's.

One of the things Russell talked about in his opening talk was having things for people who aren't ready yet. He taught that we need to ascend them up what he calls 'The Value Ladder', over time, to create the most meaningful impact.

He spent the next few minutes discussing the principles, and at the next break, I jumped into my email system to see how I could apply this newfound insight. It was already starting to make sense because I had been offering my prospective clients the same thing over and over again. Just like Russell said, eventually those things begin to have a 'diminishing value' until they have none at all.

Technically, I was right with my partner, but not in the right way. I realized that what I needed to do was make the approach to the webinar more gradual. Jumping from zero to "come to this webinar now" was like asking my prospective clients to climb up the North Face of the Eiger, an impossibly steep upward climb that only few were ready to embark upon. My solution was too static and linear, meant for a single point of transaction only when the timing and circumstances were nearly perfect for it. This was why my 3,000 strong email list was barely converting 1.00% into recurring webinar attendees.

At the end of his session, I skipped the next one to work on creating my own ascent for our prospective clients but my mind was completely blank. "Do I just make more webinars?" I pondered as I felt like the dumbest person in the empty virtual room I was still 'standing' in.

I spent the rest of the day in turmoil over what I was supposed to do with all of this information, financial services are so regulated that there was no way I could do all the things other businesses do in terms of marketing. How could I possibly ascend people when I just need to get them in "the process"?

While I was stressing about this, upset, I skipped the next session just to sit around with zero good ideas. I hopped back into the conference and figured I'd think about this later when I had time to process it. About halfway through the next presentation, the answer came to me. It was something that for unknown reasons, I just "knew".

What I knew at that moment was that I didn't need to redo my offer because it wasn't good enough. I needed to expand my understanding of what an offer was, and how to give different ones to different people, based on where they were on their journey.

This meant that I wasn't going to make 10 different webinars, although that could be a solution that is viable long-term. I needed something today. It meant that I needed something for someone who wasn't ready to commit to spending 45 to 90 minutes on a webinar, and I also needed to design something for people who had already benefited from our financial service offer.

So, I got to work and built out a series of high-value content affectionately known as "lead magnets" to provide value to people on my email list who weren't ready, in much shorter bites. These were PDF guides, checklists, whitepapers, and podcast episodes I hosted with a CPA friend who later helped us build the path for our clients to ascend even higher by providing tax services with our own company.

Within weeks of this shift, I redid the copywriting on the previous webinar we had done 50 times already and relaunched our campaign.

The results were astounding. Not only did sign-ups triple from previous webinars with the same exact content, the attendance rate for sign-ups was nearly 80%. The only thing I did differently was add the "bread crumbs" for people to follow up the trail to the summit of our offer. Because I did this, we had an influx of clients who never would have found us otherwise.

The only thing I did was add critical steps early in the journey to get people started. Because of this serious influx of clients and business, I was afforded even more opportunity to take time and improve our mousetrap. Within 6 months, our webinar attendance regularly held at 50+ and we opened an Outside Business Activity (OBA) that three financial advisors owned, to provide tax & accounting services. We didn't work in it; we just owned it and outsourced the work to a CPA who did business under our banner. This dual strategy meant that there were multiple entry points into our business that could easily cross-sell to the other.

That's exactly what happened! Today, that tax & accounting business is approaching $1 million dollars in subscription-based revenue (we opted not to do hourly rates and did monthly subscription instead), while our financial advisory practice is so solid that I was able to step away to pursue marketing full-time.

This is the power of The Value Ascent that you will create for your clients; it can change everything.

In our business, we deal in trust. It's the only way anything intangible, like the concept of a robust financial future, can be sold. To build trust with this kind of offer is way easier than other offers, but it will only work, just like any offer, when the timing is right.

It's one of the biggest reasons that we "drip" on clients with emails and calls. If you've ever done this you probably also found that the reason it took so long was just that they weren't ready, for one reason or another.

You can continue to do that if you wish, but with some intention you can 10x the value of your interactions, and you guessed it... it involves a framework.

It is simple once you know its purpose — it's to determine 2 things:

1. What you give to or do for people who aren't ready yet.

2. What you give to or do for people who have already work with you.

Typical Advisor: A Disjointed Approach

Many financial advisors fall into the trap of doing a bunch of disconnected activities that don't add up to a cohesive strategy. Here's how a typical advisor might operate:

- **Social Media Posts:** Posting sporadically on different platforms without a clear plan or consistent messaging.

- **Sporadic Emails:** Sending out emails at random intervals with no follow-up or cohesive narrative, leading to inconsistent engagement.

- **LinkedIn Campaign:** Launching a LinkedIn campaign without integrating it into a larger strategy, resulting in short-lived spikes in activity that don't convert into long-term relationships.

- **Random Videos:** Creating and sharing videos without a clear purpose or connection to other content, making it hard for clients to see the value or relevance.

- **One-Off Client Calls (OPC):** Having client calls that are not part of a structured follow-up process, leading to missed opportunities and disorganized follow-ups.

Rinse and Repeat

Advisors often repeat this cycle of disconnected activities, hoping that something will stick. This approach leads to:

- **Wasted Time and Resources:** Investing effort in activities that don't yield sustainable results.

- **Inconsistent Client Engagement:** Failing to build a steady relationship due to the lack of a coherent strategy.

- **Lost Opportunities:** Missing chances to convert leads into clients because the approach is too fragmented.

Even for the most ambitious marketer/advisor, this lack of focus and intentionality makes this work, very hard work.

Given a likely and frustrating run through compliance and little results, it's easy to just say marketing doesn't work, and you'd be right this kind doesn't. The reason is actually far less insidious than you think and I'll explain what happened to all of us.

Up until the Global Financial crisis of 2008, the industry was a bit like the Wild West (it's the reason it happened) and regulations around what was suitable for someone was pretty lax, particularly around statements later deemed to be "promising". Suffice it to say, bad things happened and like most regulatory interventions, there was an overcorrection and all the big firms got a talking to and were then responsible for everything their people ever said or did.

This brought on a slew of rules and regulations enforceable at the FINRA and SEC level, punishable by hefty fines. To create a buffer for this, firms adopted stricter policies and the government bails you out. Make no mistake, this is an acquisition made by the government; what they're acquiring is control. They don't need money; they can print it.

So, what happens when government controlled, highly regulated organizations get put in charge of marketing departments? Marketing dies — at least the kind of marketing that works. The type of marketing that gets approved is the kind that the big firms know how to do (albeit, not very well) — corporate brand marketing. The problem is, the way you market a Fortune 500 company with 50+ years of market presence is basically the opposite from how you market an individual brand that has very little.

Let me explain. Imagine you work for Coca-Cola and you've just been hired to promote a brand new sparkling water. Would it really be that hard knowing that the other billion dollar products will do most of the work for you? Nope, which is why they do a couple of social media posts that took a 12 person marketing team two weeks to make, with a 6-7 figure ad budget. This same philosophy is pushed down to our level as financial advisors and professionals, except that their ego got in the way, making them think the brand name is enough.

Think about it — what has any piece of marketing advice to you ever been?

- Increase exposure
- Expand awareness
- Provide education

"Go places and tell people what you do. Everyone needs financial advice and they trust our brand. So, it's practically a given," said every marketer in a home office, ever.

We like to call this "echelons above reality" where decisions are made by those who have never been in our shoes or have been out for so long they've forgotten. So, until I become the President of Marketing for the U.S. (maybe that's the FCC?) we can deal with this obstacle, or we can bypass it. Let's explore the second and find a new way.

The new path is to create a journey up your value mountain, but it can't be straight to the summit, few people will be ready right away. Remember it is in the hero's nature to refuse the call to action initially, so we need to build in some "switchbacks" to help climbers get to the top. Switchbacks are those zig zagging trails that lead up to the top. This helps climbers and hikers walk a less direct path to the top — one they could navigate much more easily than the direct route.

For example, on a hiking trip to Mt. Whitney in 2017 with my brother, we traversed 99 switchbacks to the top. Without them, we would have been forced to walk directly up which was outside of the skills and ability of our group.

So let's start with your Atomic offer, which is not the summit, draw a mountain and put it halfway up, this is base camp. Firstly, let's find some routes to basecamp. How do people get to your offer or basecamp?

That's right! As the master sherpa of our offer, we should know all of the routes up and down the mountain. To attract people who may not have the comfort level or awareness to the full value of your offer.

We need to offer some easier routes up. By doing this, we shift from having a single point of sale that everything is riding on and, instead, allow people to get the "snack sized" version of your offer. This is how you warm people up, and keep them on ice until they're ready for you. To do this, we essentially need to make some content, but not just any content; high value content.

What's high value content?

It's carefully crafted or curated content that speaks directly to your hero. "High value" is a relative term; these are also called lead magnets. They appear to be so specific and valuable that your hero will part with their precious personal email address and/or phone number —knowing that they'll get added to a sequence — because they feel they need it.

There are many ways to do this effectively. Depending on your skillset, we'll start with easy wins and go to more effective ones. These are truly the secret weapons for your brand. So, take the time to get it right, but most importantly, get started.

Secret Weapon #1: The Challenger — There are few things in this world that bring more satisfaction than setting out to accomplish something difficult and then actually doing it.

This is why "challenges" work. Optimally ranging from 7-14 days, every day, you'll ask your hero to take a small step towards their goal.

Here are some easy ones to do:

- 7 Day Portfolio Challenge: Every day, ask them to review one portfolio metric.

- 14 Day Financial Planning Challenge: Every day, ask them to organize one area of their financial life

Here's an example of what a 7-Day Portfolio Challenge could look like:

7-Day Portfolio Mastery Challenge

Join our 7-Day Portfolio Mastery Challenge and transform your understanding of investment portfolios. Over the next week, you'll gain the knowledge and tools you need to confidently manage and optimize your investments. Whether you're a seasoned investor or just starting out, this challenge will help you take control of your financial future.

Day 1: Portfolio Basics

Objective: Understand the foundational elements of an investment portfolio.

- **Introduction to Investment Portfolios:** Learn what an investment portfolio is and why it's important.

- **Components of a Portfolio:** Stocks, bonds, mutual funds, ETFs, and other assets.

- **Risk and Return:** Basics of how risk and return work together.

- **Activity:** Create a list of all your current investments.

Outcome: Gain a clear understanding of what makes up a portfolio and why diversification matters.

Day 2: Assessing Your Current Portfolio

Objective: Evaluate the current state of your investment portfolio.

- **Portfolio Evaluation Techniques:** How to assess your portfolio's performance.

- **Analyzing Asset Allocation:** Understand your current mix of assets.

- **Identifying Strengths and Weaknesses:** Spot areas that need improvement.

- **Activity:** Use a simple tool to analyze your current portfolio's allocation and performance.

Outcome: Develop a comprehensive view of where your portfolio stands today.

Day 3: Diversification and Risk Management

Objective: Learn strategies to diversify and manage risk effectively.

- **The Importance of Diversification:** How spreading your investments can reduce risk.

- **Types of Diversification:** Across asset classes, sectors, and geographies.

- **Risk Management Techniques:** Ways to protect your portfolio from market volatility.

- **Activity:** Adjust your portfolio to improve diversification based on the day's lessons.

Outcome: Implement strategies to create a balanced and resilient portfolio.

Day 4: Setting Investment Goals

Objective: Define clear, achievable investment goals.

- **Short-term vs. Long-term Goals:** Understand the difference and why both are important.

- **SMART Goals Framework:** Setting Specific, Measurable, Achievable, Relevant, Time-bound goals.

- **Aligning Goals with Portfolio Strategy:** How to ensure your investments support your financial objectives.

- **Activity:** Write down your top three investment goals and align them with your current portfolio strategy.

Outcome: Clear investment goals that guide your portfolio management decisions.

Day 5: Performance Tracking and Adjustment

Objective: Learn how to track portfolio performance and make necessary adjustments.

- **Key Performance Metrics:** Understand important metrics like ROI, CAGR, and volatility.

- **Regular Portfolio Reviews:** The importance of consistent performance tracking.

- **Making Adjustments:** When and how to rebalance your portfolio.

- **Activity:** Set up a performance tracking system using a spreadsheet or financial software.

Outcome: Develop a routine for monitoring and adjusting your portfolio to stay on track with your goals.

Day 6: Tax Efficiency and Costs

Objective: Optimize your portfolio for tax efficiency and cost-effectiveness.

- **Tax-Advantaged Accounts:** Learn about IRAs, 401(k)s, and other tax-advantaged accounts.

- **Tax-Efficient Investment Strategies:** How to minimize tax liabilities.

- **Understanding Fees:** Identify and reduce investment costs and fees.

- **Activity:** Review your portfolio for tax efficiency and hidden fees, and make adjustments as needed.

Outcome: A more tax-efficient and cost-effective portfolio.

Day 7: Building a Long-Term Strategy

Objective: Create a long-term investment strategy for sustained success.

- **Developing a Long-Term Plan:** How to create a strategy that evolves with your life stages and market conditions.

- **Staying Informed:** Keeping up with market trends and adjusting your strategy.

- **Dealing with Market Changes:** Strategies to stay calm and proactive during market fluctuations.

- **Activity:** Write down your long-term investment strategy, including how you will stay informed and make adjustments over time.

Outcome: A robust long-term investment strategy that adapts to your evolving financial needs and market conditions.

These are basic, but you can add your own spin on it, or even get more granular.

10 Day Back to School College Planning Challenge: Every day, send emails asking them to do one thing.

Here's an example:

10-Day Back to School College Planning Challenge Overview

Join our 10-Day Back to School College Planning Challenge and get your finances in order for college. Each day, you'll receive an email with a specific task designed to help you plan and prepare for college expenses. By the end of the challenge, you'll have a comprehensive plan to manage college costs effectively.

Day 1: Set Your Financial Goals

Email Subject: Day 1: Set Your Financial Goals for College

Objective: Define clear, achievable financial goals for college.

Email Content: Welcome to Day 1 of the College Planning Challenge! Today, we'll focus on setting your financial goals. Think about what you want to achieve, financially, during college. Do you want to graduate debt-free? Save a specific amount each year? Write down your top three financial goals and keep them somewhere visible.

Task: Write down your top three financial goals for college and place them where you can see them daily.

Day 2: Estimate College Costs

Email Subject: Day 2: Estimate Your College Costs.

Objective: Get a clear picture of the total cost of college.

Email Content: Today, let's estimate the total cost of your college education. Research the tuition, fees, room and board, books, and other expenses for your chosen colleges. Use online calculators or resources to get accurate estimates.

Task: Create a list of estimated costs for each college you're considering.

Day 3: Explore Financial Aid Options

Email Subject: Day 3: Explore Your Financial Aid Options

Objective: Understand the different types of financial aids available.

Email Content: It's time to explore financial aid options! Learn about grants, scholarships, work-study programs, and loans. Check out the financial aid websites of your chosen colleges and start making a list of potential aid sources.

Task: List at least five financial aid options you can pursue.

Day 4: Complete the FAFSA

Email Subject: Day 4: Complete Your FAFSA

Objective: Start the FAFSA application process.

Email Content: Filling out the Free Application for Federal Student Aid (FAFSA) is crucial for accessing financial aid. Gather the necessary documents (tax returns, W-2s, etc.) and begin the application process.

Task: Start your FAFSA application today.

Day 5: Search for Scholarships

Email Subject: Day 5: Start Your Scholarship Search

Objective: Find and apply for scholarships.

Email Content: Scholarships can significantly reduce your college costs. Use scholarship search engines and resources to find scholarships you're eligible for. Remember, every dollar counts!

Task: Apply for at least three scholarships today.

Day 6: Create a Budget

Email Subject: Day 6: Create Your College Budget

Objective: Develop a budget to manage your college expenses.

Email Content: Creating a budget helps you to manage your money effectively. List your income sources (financial aid, part-time job, etc.) and expenses (tuition, books, living expenses). Make sure your budget balances and allows for savings.

Task: Create a detailed budget for your first year of college.

Day 7: Plan for Emergency Funds

Email Subject: Day 7: Plan Your Emergency Fund

Objective: Set up an emergency fund for unexpected expenses.

Email Content: Having an emergency fund is crucial. Aim to save at least $500 to cover unexpected expenses like medical bills or car repairs. This fund can provide peace of mind during your college years.

Task: Set a goal and start building your emergency fund today.

Day 8: Learn About Student Loans

Email Subject: Day 8: Understand Student Loans

Objective: Get informed about student loan options and responsibilities.

Email Content: Student loans can be a useful tool but come with responsibilities. Learn about the types of loans available, interest rates, repayment options, and how to borrow wisely.

Task: Research and list the pros and cons of different student loan options.

Day 9: Plan for Part-Time Work

Email Subject: Day 9: Explore Part-Time Work Opportunities

Objective: Find ways to earn money while studying.

Email Content: Working part-time can help you manage expenses and gain valuable experience. Look for on-campus jobs, internships, or freelance work that fit your schedule and interests.

Task: Apply for at least two part-time job opportunities.

Day 10: Review and Adjust Your Plan

Email Subject: Day 10: Review and Finalize Your College Plan

Objective: Review your entire college plan and make any necessary adjustments.

Email Content: Congratulations on completing the challenge! Today, review all the steps you've taken and adjust your plan as needed. Make sure your goals, budget, and financial aid applications are all in order.

Task: Review your college financial plan and make any final adjustments.

Additionally, you'll see I added a time component that implies scarcity. In our industry, this is a tight rope. We can't say things like "limited seats; less than 10 left" because attorneys and compliance analysts think that somehow contributes to liability using their extensive experience in sales and marketing.

I once couldn't use the word "propulsion" because it was deemed promissory, despite my reference to Webster's definition of the word, stating that it means to move forward, not up. So, to avoid trying to teach an attorney or compliance analyst about marketing (you can't), we'll take the long way.

"Back to school", "end of year", and other time gates imply the same scarcity, (that this offer, in this configuration, is limited). That's the key. Firms get all weird about marketing their stuff, but remember that most are clueless about how to market individual service brands, and by some, I mean all. When your atomic offer shows up, who are they to say what is or isn't true? Use this to your advantage, this book puts you in control now.

Secret Weapon #2

In addition to accomplishing something tough, humans will do almost anything to avoid stepping on a land mine if they can help it. We're talking basic survival here. This is best done with a lot of curiosity. Too often, I see too much given away, satisfying people's curiosity and allowing them to move on without taking action. Here's what I mean:

Not curious: "Exploring how the CARES Act can impact your retirement."

This sucks and was definitely written by a compliance analyst pretending to know marketing– zero people will download this.

Remember, how to or X ways to [Do Good/Avoid Bad], finally [solve main problem], get [aspirational goal], and stop [internal problem] for good without dealing with [external problem].

Examples:

Example 1: "7 Ways to Bulletproof Your Retirement Savings from Unexpected Legislation Changes, Achieve Peace of Mind, and Eliminate Financial Anxiety Without Navigating Complex Legal Jargon."

Example 2: "How to Maximize Your 401(k) Returns in a Volatile Market, Secure Your Financial Future, and End Market Stress Without Becoming a Market Expert."

Example 3: "5 Secret Tricks to Protect Your Investments from Tax Hikes, Capital Gains Nightmares, and Alleviate Worries About Future Taxation Without Complicated Tax Planning or Paying Your CPA an Arm and a Leg."

Secret Weapon #3: The Follow Up Sequence

As an advisor, you've probably heard that it takes anywhere from 10 to 25 touchpoints before people become clients. What I'm going to tell you now is that there is no point being clever if you can't be lazy too — and now, it's time to become a clever fox. You can automate these touchpoints, and here's how we do that — the follow-up sequence.

Character Accelerator Sequence (CAS):

The Character Accelerator Sequence (CAS) is designed to quickly build rapport and showcase your personality to new subscribers. Over the course of 5 days, you'll send a series of emails that introduce yourself, share your story, and provide valuable insights that resonate with your audience.

Example CAS:

Day 1: Welcome and Introduction

- Subject: "Welcome! Here's What You Can Expect"
- Content: Introduce yourself, share your mission, and what subscribers can expect from your emails. Include a personal story that highlights your values and approach.

Day 2: Your Origin Story

- Subject: "How I Got Started in Financial Services"
- Content: Share your journey into financial services, including challenges and successes. This helps build a personal connection.

Day 3: Overcoming Challenges

- Subject: "The Biggest Financial Mistake I Made (And How You Can Avoid It)"
- Content: Discuss a significant challenge you faced and overcame. Offer actionable advice to help your audience avoid the same pitfalls.

Day 4: Client Success Story

- Subject: "How [Client's Name] Transformed Their Financial Future"

- Content: Highlight a client's success story that showcases your expertise and the impact of your services. Include testimonials if possible.

Day 5: Valuable Resource

- Subject: "Your Free Guide to Financial Freedom"

- Content: Provide a valuable resource (e.g., an e-book or checklist) that helps your audience take the next step in their financial journey. Reinforce your commitment to their success.

Trust Accelerator Sequence (TAS):

The Trust Accelerator Sequence (TAS) is spread over 24 days with 8-12 emails sent 2-3 days apart. This sequence aims to build trust and deepen the relationship by providing valuable content, insights, and addressing common concerns.

Example TAS:

Email 1: Educational Content

- Subject: "The Top 5 Financial Myths Debunked"

- Content: Provide educational content that addresses common misconceptions and offers clarity.

Email 2: Case Study

- Subject: "How We Helped [Client's Name] Achieve Their Financial Goals"

- Content: Share a detailed case study of a client who achieved success through your services.

Email 3: Addressing Pain Points

- Subject: "Worried About Market Volatility? Here's What You Need to Know"

- Content: Address a common pain point and offer actionable advice to mitigate concerns.

Email 4: Behind-the-Scenes

- Subject: "A Day in the Life of a Financial Advisor"

- Content: Give a behind-the-scenes look at your work process and how you help clients.

Email 5: FAQ

- Subject: "Your Most Asked Questions Answered"

- Content: Address frequently asked questions to clear up any doubts or misconceptions.

Email 6: Free Consultation Offer

- Subject: "Ready to Take the Next Step? Let's Talk"

- Content: Offer a free consultation to discuss their financial goals and how you can help.

Email 7: Value-Added Content

- Subject: "How to Create a Bulletproof Retirement Plan"
- Content: Provide in-depth content that offers significant value and practical advice.

Email 8: Call to Action

- Subject: "Don't Miss Out on Your Financial Transformation"
- Content: Encourage them to take action, whether it's scheduling a consultation or downloading additional resources.

Need Identification (NID):

The Need Identification Sequence (NID) is a one-day process where you send a survey to new leads to personalize their experience. This helps you to understand their specific needs and tailor your content accordingly.

Example NID:

Day 1: Personalized Survey

- Subject: "Help Us to Help You Better – Quick Survey Inside"

- Content: Send a survey asking key questions about their financial goals, challenges, and preferences. Use this information to segment your audience and provide personalized content.

Survey Questions:

1. What are your top three financial goals?

2. What financial challenges are you currently facing?

3. How do you prefer to receive financial advice (e.g., email, video, phone)?

4. What topics are you most interested in learning about?

This framework will form the base of your initial communications. I know that as financial advisors we can feel weird about marketing but it's only because of how the industry and the media convinced you to view yourself.

So often, I hear things like, "You should run your office like a doctor's office." That might sound really cool but here's the deal — you didn't go to school for 8 years and get 4 to 6 years of on-the-job training before you were allowed to practice, so don't put yourself on this pedestal; you haven't earned that.

That's not the worst part of that phrase though; have you been to a doctor's office recently? They're usually overbooked, understaffed and the doctors see you as dollar signs. Typically, they are at least 10-15 minutes late to their own appointments, and that's being generous. One time, I sat in my doctor's office for 45 minutes, waiting for her to arrive for a routine annual physical, and while I was waiting, I received a call from her asking why I did not show up to my appointment.

I'd switch doctors but my experience would probably be the same. So, let's honor that while being "like a" doctor or attorney makes you believe that you sound cooler, if anyone ever told me they run their practice like a doctor's office, I wouldn't say anything back; I'd just stand up and walk out.

You're a business person, building a business. Despite who you are, what you are, and how you serve, this is the best positioning for yourself, from an approach perspective. You are you. Your offer is yours; your experience is unique. Don't set yourself up for failure by trying to position yourself in a seemingly elevated role that could create discontent. The other thing it does is to liken the outcomes to theirs — variable, free from accountability, lengthy, and often costly.

The reason I say this is because of frequency apprehension. You're never, ever, going to get clients by emailing them once a week, for years, on end, until you appeal to their appreciation for persistence. As soon as someone has expressed interest in your offer, it means they understand their problem and that you can be the solution.

This means that you need to hit the throttle.

The only reason I give anything away for downloads online is exchange for emails, I then use those emails to get the user to my funnel or what you're about to learn that I call "The Perfect Mouse Trap". If they don't take me up on it and unsubscribe from my emails, they're doing me a favor because most email systems charge by contacts, not email sends.

The sole purpose of all of your emails, posts, etc., is to get the user to your offer. Period. Period. Period.

In the examples above, I was nice and spread them out over 2-3 days each to have a nice monthly communication plan, but as soon as someone downloads something and gives me their email, they're going to get emailed with five CAS emails, and 25 TAS emails over the course of 30 days.

I don't care if they don't like it; they agreed to it when they took my valuable offer to download my content.

That's like someone signing up for the gym and getting mad when someone encourages them every day to push themselves and do more. If they aren't going to act on your CTAs that get them to your offer within the first 30 days, either segment them for nurturing campaigns or delete them entirely (which is what I do). If I want to throw the hook out in the future to catch them again when they're ready, I can.

7

Build The Perfect Mousetrap

If you don't do anything else in this book, you absolutely need to do this part.

Let me tell you why.

Russell Brunson's $3.2M Story

Russell Brunson, the founder of ClickFunnels, took the stage at Grant Cardone's 10x event in Vegas. The room was packed with thousands of entrepreneurs, all eager to learn how to scale their businesses. Russell didn't just share strategies; he told his story, mixing personal experiences with actionable insights.

He guided the audience through a journey, showing them the potential for their own businesses. When he introduced his product, it was with a clear, compelling offer that resonated deeply. He knew their needs and fears, addressing them directly. The room buzzed with excitement.

By the end of his presentation, Russell had generated $3.2 million in sales, in just 90 minutes. This was no accident. It was the result of careful planning and understanding his audience. His message hit the mark.

Russell's success at the 10x event wasn't just about the money. It was about the impact he made. He changed the way those entrepreneurs thought, gave them hope, and provided a clear path to their goals.

This story highlights the power of a well-crafted presentation. When you connect deeply with your audience and make an irresistible offer, you achieve extraordinary results. If you take one thing from this book, let it be this: master your message and craft offers your audience cannot resist. Just like Russell Brunson, you can achieve incredible success and make a lasting impact.

We're going to use the same thing. You'll find that all of the work you have done so far will help you greatly here so it's really just a matter of putting the pieces together in a very powerful way.

I'll show you the framework and then cover each aspect of it. We won't go into too much technical detail, to keep it evergreen, meaning you can use this for a:

- 90 minute webinar/seminar

- 60 minute webinar/seminar

- 30 minute webinar/seminar

- 15 minute conversation

- 5 minute webinar ad

- 60 second short

You can also repurpose it for:

- E-books

- Social media

- Lead magnets

- Blog articles

- Brochures

- Fliers

It's not just a perfect webinar; it serves multiple purposes and can be configured to catch anything, anywhere.

Retention	1. Getting Them To Stay
Receptive	2. Breaking Down False Beliefs
	3. Rebuilding New True Beliefs w/ offer
Realization	4. Increase value of offer (presell)

Reaction	5. Position your offer w/ CTA cycle

This is the perfect mousetrap. Here's how it works in the simplest way, so that you understand what's happening:

1. **Hook + Big Promise:** Capture attention with a strong hook and a big promise.

2. **What You'll Learn:** Provide clear value by telling them what they'll learn.

3. **Who It's For:** Qualify your audience by explaining who the webinar is for.

4. **Who It's Not For / What It's Not:** Address objections by stating who it's not for and what it's not.

5. **Stay Till the End:** Offer a payoff to keep them engaged until the end.

Backstory: Establish credibility, empathy, and authority with your personal story.

Trials and Epiphany: Share the challenges you faced and the moment of insight that led to your success.

Success: Highlight your achievements and how you overcame obstacles.

Before/After: Show transformation and provide proof with before and after examples.

Big Domino / 2 Choices: Be clear about what you want them to achieve, presenting it as a clear choice.

Secret #1: Your vehicle to the destination. Explain your process and agreement.

- **False Belief 1:** "I don't have enough time to focus on marketing while managing my clients."

- **False Belief 2:** "I don't have the technical skills needed to run effective marketing campaigns."

- **False Belief 3:** "Marketing is too expensive and doesn't provide a good return on investment."

Secret #2: Get rid of limiting internal beliefs. Eliminate external and villain limiting beliefs.

- **False Belief 1:** "I don't know where to start with my marketing efforts."

- **False Belief 2:** "My clients won't appreciate me spending time on marketing."

- **False Belief 3:** "I've tried marketing before, and it didn't work for me."

Secret #3: Address external problems and the villain limiting beliefs. Focus on obstacles outside their control and how to overcome them.

- **False Belief 1:** "There are too many regulations and compliance issues in financial marketing."
- **False Belief 2:** "Big firms have too much market share for me to compete."
- **False Belief 3:** "The marketing landscape changes too quickly for me to keep up."

Transition to Presale:

Check Ride: Ensure they're with you and build momentum.

Offer: Present your offer, one slide at a time. Discuss the perceived and qualitative value as it relates to their lives. Money is not the only currency in our lives: time, cumulative stress, and sustained energy are also currencies. Recap the offer, emphasizing how it delivers 10x the value.

If you have a monetized price for your offer ($2,500 for a financial plan, for example) the components leading up to it should make them feel like they're getting $25,000 worth of stuff. There are a lot of nuances to that in our industry, and I have found that you don't need to monetize the value as much because I faced similar difficulties getting this concept approved, deleted it and rolled with it anyway. It worked just as well as I expected it to, with the monetized offer.

It's almost like cheating with these offers because your competitors' marketing, even at Fortune level firms, are terrible. I'm still so amazed at how bad they are. So, you're in good shape just by using this framework, regardless of what you get approved to show.

Transition to Selling:

1. **CTA 1 – Purpose:** Explain why they are here and what they can achieve.

2. **CTA 2 – Value:** Highlight the value by asking, "If all this did was..."

3. **CTA 3 – Potential:** Future pace and help them imagine the potential.

4. **CTA Inf. (Optional) – Q&A:** Offer a Q&A session, stating that some might be one question away from clarity.

You can shrink or expand it, and as long as ratios stay the same of ⅓, ⅓, ⅓ you can use it anywhere.

The method mechanics behind this are relatively straightforward; you're using nearly every aspect of psychology-based marketing to make yourself a very powerful guide worth following, and making sure that when you talk, people listen. Then you're inviting them in as the story's hero and demonstrating that you know exactly how to help them get what they want without the pain.

You can't guess at objections, so you have to address all of them as you go. Once they see all of their false beliefs and accept them, you position your offer as the solution. Finally, you're addressing the widest set of objections possible, in different ways, so they finally take action <u>now</u>.

Depending on where/how you deploy your mousetrap, even for those that don't convert via webinar, you'll remarket and retarget them afterwards, continuing to build and foster your community until they're ready.

After the webinar/event you can:

- Send follow up emails encouraging them to take action
- Check in to see how they liked the "payoff" gift
- Send a survey — content quality
- Send a survey — traffic score
- Invite them up the mountain with new stuff
- Add more value to your tribe offer
- Invite them to challenges

- Give exclusive content to get feedback on

- Showcase your community commitment

- Increase your halo size

- Get ideas for new stuff

- Further refine your hero through personalization

- Send recordings/exclusive content

Even though I recommend no less than 25 live iterations before moving to anything prerecorded, you can repurpose recording into highlight reels to put on your website or Youtube/Facebook channel and transform transcripts into content.

With "evergreen" intentions, I won't mention specific tools to use. However, as you get more acquainted with my approach you'll find that I am an avid user and proprietor of AI tools and creations which I'll add to the appendix for you to check out.

We'll cover the embrace of AI at the end — it's going to change your life. For now, just know this is possible:

- Transform a 30-minute video into 10-20 optimized YouTube shorts.

- Use your video transcript to identify blog topics, and get an AI tool to write them for you.

- Get feedback on your presentation based on your transcript.

- Use your transcript to get ideas and copy for social posts.

- And more.

I hope you're getting this because you can see that you are literally building a brand that feels like 500 people work there — but it's just you. Once you're done constructing your perfect mousetrap, you'll realize this is all you will ever need:

- If you add an offer, build a mousetrap.

- If you want to find a new market entry point, build a mousetrap.

- If you find out you're speaking to 10,000 people next month, build a mousetrap.

Want to grow and scale?

- Hire new people and build their mousetrap.

- Automate your mousetrap.

What else can your Perfect Mousetrap (PMT) do?

- Expand the concepts and go more in-depth to make the ultimate credibility factor.

- Boost your 'thought leadership' factor.

This is also known as a "utility book" and it's in fact, what you're reading now. It's not supposed to be the result of a life's work or some Russian novel, so don't overthink it, and also this is the step you take once everything is done. When you are ready for this step, here's a really easy way to do it without ever getting writer's block.

This book was ideated, outlined, structured, written, and edited within 30 days, and I'm a busy guy — so, it's doable.

How to Expand Your Mousetrap

There are two primary methods. Here's how you do it:

Method 1: Expand Your Content into Individual Concepts

Translate your content into individual concepts, with each chapter focusing on a specific idea. Here's a suggested structure:

- **Forward:** Backstory/Promise
- **Chapter 1:** The Big Domino
- **Chapter 2:** The Vehicle (Your Thing)
- **Chapter 3:** False Beliefs 1/2/3
- **Chapter 4:** Internal/Philosophical Problem
- **Chapter 5:** False Beliefs 1/2/3

- **Chapter 6:** External/Villain Problem
- **Chapter 7:** False Beliefs 1/2/3
- **Chapter 8:** Offer Stack
- **Chapter 9:** Call to Action 1/2/3
- **Chapter 10:** Frequently Asked Questions (F.A.Q.)
- **Bonus Tip:** Each chapter should be about 10 pages or roughly 2,500 words for a 5x7 softcover. But don't worry; you don't need to be Hemingway. I'll show you how to do it with AI soon.

We'll call this the "Mousetrap Expansion Method".

The next method, and the one I used to write this, is called the "Secret Ingredient Method". It will make your book– should you choose to write it–much more multi-functional. How you do this, is defined your "Big Domino" or the "one thing" they need to believe that takes care of everything else. We don't need to convince people to buy life insurance, if we first convince them they need a holistic financial plan, because life insurance is included in a holistic financial plan — feel me?

So, let's say I want to use my book to sell more financial plans, or sell them for more, or both. We'll ignore leveling up the copy for this example, so you can see the bones.

Title: Financial Planning Secrets

Subtitle: Discover the 9 Pillars of Building an All-Weather Plan That Your Financial Advisor Doesn't Want You To Know

You can just start there; we know what we're making now.

Now, let's create the pillars. Don't assume that the first 9 things you think of are bangers, because they probably aren't. Write out in a stack what you believe the pillars are and be sure to put down 12-15 things. They could be things like:

"Save 20% of What You Earn"

"Put All-Weather Tires on your Portfolio"

"Never Pay Taxes Twice"

"Diversify Intelligently"

"Allocate Correctly"

"Get Appropriate Insurance"

"Protect from Creditors/Predators"

Once you have them all down, just like filmmakers do, we need to remove anything not relevant to the story. So, explore how to combine or eliminate the unnecessary to ensure that we have the 9 pillars. Underneath each of the 9 things, write down 5-7 questions someone might ask about the pillar.

For example: "Save 20% of What You Earn"

- "How is that even possible?"
- "What about my lifestyle?"
- "What if something happens?"
- "How is this sustainable?"
- "How long does it take?"
- "What about my debt"

Then we'll turn these into statements that hook the reader and answer the questions for "Save 20% of What You Earn".

- The secret trick to make saving more easy
- How to keep your life the same, even as you save more
- Preventing unexpected events from ruining your saving potential
- The key to long term sustainable savings growth
- The impact of saving now versus later
- Why paying off debt first could ruin your future

Think about it; do you see any other financial advisor books out there like this? Now, imagine a book with your name and face on it, filled with 10-12 chapters and over 50 secret ingredients. Do this and you'll have a business card that will never be thrown away, and if you're really good, you can get other people to pay to publish your book.

I know! Let me explain really quick, but this is where your tribe comes in (more on this soon). As a financial advisor, you probably know CPAS, attorneys, P&C agents, bankers, real estate agents, lenders, consultants, and more — these are who you hit up.

How you get them to pay for it is by pre-ordering copies of your book in exchange for a full page ad in the back of your book. Give it to them at cost. If it's $9 a book, to have 1,000 copies made, that's $9,000 for a print run. Figure out how many people will buy and divide your offer up, keeping 50 or so for yourself.

By doing this, you not only got your book published for free, you also just put 950 copies of your book into the hands of the tribe that wants you to be successful.

Why Will They Give it to Clients and Why Does This Work so Well?

1. You just gave them 100 copies of a book they only need 1 of.

2. They are showcased in the book that they are giving away.

3. It is counter-culture to throw books away (people just don't do it).

It's almost diabolical how well it works, except that everyone wins. It's just awesome! That's how to build the "Perfect Mousetrap" to use quickly, and then scale it with lightning speed.

8

BUILD YOUR TRIBE

Early on in my career as a financial advisor, I got some really bad advice about networking and meeting people. The guidance I received was that I should just meet as many people as possible and ask them to do business with me.

Have you ever gotten this advice? It's stupid, I know.

I was told to join a Business Network International (BNI) group, a Rotary Club, or all of the associations, or go to networking events randomly to sift through the sea of broke entrepreneurs to find someone I could help.

The problem with this is, I'm not very extraverted. In fact, the idea of going to those things and talking to strangers for undetermined amounts of time, with nearly infinite permutations of what conversations could arise, gets me pretty close to panic attack territory. I'm just an introverted person, and when I interact with people, it comes at the expense of my energy levels.

My introversion and spending most of my adult life abroad, in the military, meant that when I started, I had a net zero natural market. This caused a lot of stress and anxiety for me because how in the world is an introverted person with no natural market going to head off to all of these events and come back with the gold?

During this phase of my journey, the truth was that I avoided them like the plague and it was the worst thing I could have done. Since beginning this career, I have learned again and again the value of interactions and relationships with other people. So, for the sake of your business, do not skip this part. It is essential for the road ahead, but not for the reasons you might think.

You aren't building a tribe to get referrals. Those are great to receive, but you can't count on those, and you can't rely on others to build your business for you — some of the right people can help you build it faster than you, and even they understand.

This happened to me when I started to build relationships with external service providers to my ideal clients, dentists. We got asked by a company that provides cloud recruiting services to dental offices to hop on a webinar and present information to their audience. Their whole strategy was to add as much value in as many ways as possible for their audience, even if it didn't relate to their specific solutions. It was such a good idea that we immediately jumped at it.

The first few times we did webinars with them, we had the understanding that we could promote ourselves on the webinar, and despite us asking, there was no way they were giving their email list to us. But still, we had only gotten one bite from this effort and they didn't end up becoming clients of ours in the end.

I thought to myself that there was no way it could be this difficult; I had to be missing something. What happened next changed the game in how I go to market digitally, is a staple of how I build my audience now, and will be in the future as well, because it's evergreen.

It hit me like a ton of bricks. I needed to get their audience on our website, so that I could get them to sign up for our newsletter (yes, I was embarrassingly sending newsletters at this time still). So, a couple of days before our upcoming webinar, I threw a simple landing page together that had a form to subscribe and stay up-to-date with relevant info if they liked what they saw on the webinar.

I didn't overthink it, and in fact I hated how it looked initially but knew we had to just go with it. I made an arrangement with the company we were doing these webinars for, that afterwards, if they could send out a quick email to everyone with the link to my landing page to sign up, it would be great.

They agreed, and after the webinar, I watched my inbox anxiously to make sure they didn't mess the link up or whatever scarcity minded thoughts I had racing at the time. Then, I heard the ding. I ran to my inbox and checked it. The link was perfect; let's see if this works. I knew my current Cost-Per-Lead was $6.00 after a lot of painful attempts on Facebook and Google ads, and each subscriber we got was a savings of $6.00.

Within the first few minutes, we already had 100 new subscribers to our emails, which was already a savings of over $600 in leads that I didn't have to buy.

Within the first few days, we had over 1,000. Saving us $6,000 in lead generation costs. Then, I expanded this approach to others who were out there, helping my client base to see what kind of coalition I could build up. I found 4 other people who were motivated like I was to find massive success on this journey.

Within the first few weeks, we got over 5,000 leads from external sources, saving us $30,000 in lead generation costs.

After a few months, we got over 10,000, saving us $60,000 in lead generation costs. After the first year, and through additional expanded efforts and outreach, we got 25,000 subscribers.

In the end, this strategy helped us save $150,000 in advertising expense (that honestly, my partner would have never signed off on) just by building relationships with the right kind of people. It can work for you too.

Your business can actually grow really quickly when the right people come together but it can be difficult to imagine this in an industry that typically focuses on things as individual sports. Your "tribe" could have other advisors in it; maybe you each focus on different aspects, but it will primarily be people within the sphere of influence of clients.

Typically, these guides fit very well in a financial advisors tribe, and I say "Tribe" intentionally. A tribe is distinct from a group because you all have a unified goal — the financial well-being of people. It's distinct from a family because you don't choose your family. It's distinct from a community because what benefits one doesn't always benefit all equally.

It's a tribe — brothers and sisters from another mother who come together to help protect, nurture, and grow each other's businesses. Dues are never paid to a tribe, and only one thing matters — making the tribe thrive as much as possible. Hence, this is an *active* pursuit.

I know many of you have had the same experience I have had in the past, so let's explore more about what a tribe is *not*, before discussing what is.

What a tribe is not, and who should not be in it:

- BNI Groups
- Rotary Clubs
- Vistage
- Hobby Groups
- Activity Groups
- Drinking Buddies

I say this to illuminate the reality that you do not have one, and are not in one as we sit here today. That's why the chapter is called 'tribe building', not 'tribe finding'. Tribes exist for one specific purpose, remember. So, who do you find to build a tribe with? People with an audience you want to connect with. That's it.

They could be really cool and saved you from a bear attack that one time, but unless they have an audience you want to transform into your audience, just stay friends.

Categorically, there are good potential tribe members:

- CPAs
- Attorneys
- Mortgage Lenders
- Bankers
- Real Estate Agents
- School Board Members
- Community Leaders/Boards
- Consultants
- Small Business Owners
- Social Media Influencers
- LinkedIn Thought Leaders
- Conference/Event Managers
- Podcast Hosts
- Retirement Home Coordinators
- P&C agents (Pers./Comm.)
- Health Insurance Agents
- HR Department Leaders

Every one of these people work with people in your market and probably have an audience to tap into; what your focus should be is to imbue your audience with theirs.

Let me explain why this is so critical. Unless you want to be doing weekly webinars for the next 10 years, you need an email list. The reason it's email is because you will not find anything remotely close to the effectiveness of email.

ROI on email spend is between 40-50x, depending on the industry. Nothing else you do will likely be more than 10x because of the cost/margin for error. Hence, the key to quick and monumental success is getting more traffic to your offer.

There are a few ways to get leads (and don't worry; your 'aha!' moment is coming) and 99% of advisors do #1.

1. Upload a manually or CRM generated list of leads into email tools:
   a. Bought lists
   b. Borrowed lists
   c. Recovered lists
   d. Scraped lists

Here's the deal on this — emailing people this way is not only unethical, it's illegal. Sure, you might get away with this thousands of times over. The email police are not going to come find you, but what will happen is probably much worse.

The first is that all of the work you have done will fall flat, and you will lose faith in yourself. The second is that your email domain is going to lose trust globally and tech problems arise. The third is that even if you did this to 10,000 people, it only takes one person to get an email after they unsubscribe from your list to put you at risk for $10k-$20k per infraction (and this happens — Google "Texan man makes 6 figures suing spammers"). The fourth is that any data you get will be totally useless.

So, if you're doing this, know your risks and ask yourself if it's worth it.

2. Use ads and a lead magnet to build your list

As an individual in financial services, this is where ad-based lead generation should stop, because you probably cannot cashflow an ad conversion campaign which would likely run you $10k-$12k / month to train and $5k-$7k a month to maintain, using an agency to get long-term 10-15 appointments a month.

But even so, you'll need your wallet. On Google search ads, you'll find quality leads for $7-$10 each, depending on your skills. On Facebook, since we can use images, maybe $6-$8. So, to build an effective list this way you would need:

- 3-4 lead magnets to rotate

- 3-4 ads to rotate

- Know how to use Facebook/Google ads (it's super confusing)

- Between $6K-$10K

All of that before you even send a single email.

3. Use your Tribe to build your list

Consider the 17 people I just highlighted for you to tribe build with. What if they all had only 1,000 emails each? That's 17,000 email inboxes you can get access to without spending a dime. How you do it is simple, but not easy — so, nail it before you scale it.

Add value to their clients and customers' lives, therefore, increasing their value to clients.

- For the mortgage guy: Maybe he could interview you to discuss the things he has noticed often gets people denied loans, and perhaps ask you for your advice on what people can do to maximize their chance at approval? At the end, they send a recap/recording with a link to the calendar.

I know you probably thought, this is great; I'd love other people to book meetings. But I was just kidding — do not ever do that, because the list is more valuable. How valuable is it? About $1 to $2 per person, per month. So, a list of 1,000 people should generate about $1,000 for you.

Plus, now you aren't borrowing traffic, or even controlling it; you're owning it. When you own the traffic, you've got the email. There's zero chance anyone who worked hard or paid big for a list is going to just give it to you. When they're directed to your site, you can use a squeeze page or pop-up to get their email in exchange for the checklist or whatever got promised by your tribe mater.

And that's it.

Over the last five years, tribe building has helped me curate a list of nearly 30,000 people and the math works at scale.

Building Your Tribe to Spread Your Message

Obviously, using a tribe to spread your message is the way to go. But how do we find these people and get them on the team?

Step 1: Make a List

Start by making a list of potential tribe members. These should be individuals who align with your values, have influence in your industry, and can help amplify your message.

Step 2: Engage Meaningfully Online

If your potential tribe members are online, begin by liking, commenting meaningfully, and sharing their content. Engage with their posts regularly so that when you reach out in a few weeks, it doesn't feel like a cold approach. Show genuine interest in their work and contribute to their discussions.

Step 3: Engage Offline

If they aren't active online, attend events where they are speaking or participating. After the event, send a follow-up email highlighting something specific they did that you really liked. This shows that you were paying attention and appreciated their contribution.

Step 4: Reach Out

After a few weeks of meaningful engagement, send an email or a message, reaching out. Mention the interactions you've had or the event you attended. Express your interest in discussing potential synergies and learning more about what they do to see if there's a fit for collaboration.

Step 5: Handling Rejections

Expect that most will say "no" or ignore you initially. This is totally normal and part of the process. Don't get discouraged; this is where the building starts.

Step 6: Build Slowly

Continue this process until you get one or two people to say "yes". These initial members are crucial, as they can help build credibility and attract others.

Step 7: Circle Back

Circle back to those who said "no" initially. Let them know who has joined your tribe and ask again. Mention the value and impact the tribe is already creating. The social proof will make it more likely for others to say "yes".

Step 8: Expand and Attract

Continue this process until your tribe starts to attract others on its own. The more value you provide and the stronger your network becomes, the easier it will be to grow.

Monetize Your Tribe

If you're smart, you'll find ways to monetize this further. Here are a few ideas:

- **Offer Exclusive Content:** Provide premium content or resources to tribe members.

- **Create Paid Memberships:** Charge for access to a more exclusive, inner circle of your tribe.

- **Host Paid Events:** Organize webinars, workshops, or conferences that tribe members pay to attend.

- **Collaborative Projects:** Work on joint ventures with tribe members that can be monetized.

- **Affiliate Programs:** Promote each other's services or products with a commission-based model.

By following these steps, you can effectively build a strong tribe that helps spread your message and grow your influence. The key is consistency, genuine engagement, and the provision of real value to your tribe members. Over time, this network will not only amplify your message but also open up new opportunities for collaboration and monetization.

Use the table below to begin to scoop out who you will build your tribe with. Each member should have at a minimum of 1,000 emails on their list. Don't be shy to ask what the count is.

Tribe Member Name	Profession / Market	Expected Email List Size

By the end of this, you should have at least 10,000 potential clients to get in front of, and you're coming by way of referral from trusted sources. Capture just 1.00% of this initial tribe's audience and that's 100 clients — you just made your year.

9

PUNCH IT

The #1 enemy you have, and your clients have is time. If you're rounding a corner in a racecar and you start to feel the pavement slipping out from the tires as you start to slide toward the barrier, do you know what to do? You punch it, increasing the power of your output to offset the force of gravity pulling on your car, to send you in the right direction.

This stuff is not easy, we've already discovered that. There will be many times that you'll race the circuit and it will feel different each time, but there is one distinct feeling that's always the same, and it's the slippage.

In this business, it's very hard to know what a good, or successful day is unless you got some money, because oftentimes, it's the only thing celebrated at financial services firms (no wonder we had all these problems). When I got started, I was so bad. I had just gotten out of the Army and had never sold anything in my life. I'm naturally very introverted, so the idea of walking in the heat, all day, to knock on the doors of strangers and talk to them was very hard for me to accept.

What I did discover was how good I was at coming up with reasons not to go door knocking, in my first few weeks, I had gotten less than 50 numbers. I also had no clue what I would do with the numbers I did get, which at first, were mostly numbers of lonely or elderly people at home, who gave their numbers to me because I was drenched in sweat, on their doorstep.

Pity numbers is what I got.

During this time, I was still very much a military man, walking around in my shiny $200 suit and tie combo with my dad's worn out cowboy boots from the 70's, pleather padfolio in hand, name badge clearly identifying who I am, as I took the time to wipe away the finger smudge marks for perfect appeal. I did this for weeks; it's what everyone told me to do.

Around the 4th week of the all-day, everyday door knocking, I realized that I would not have enough contacts (I'm not going to lie — I sucked; I should have gone to do something else) and I was probably going to be let go.

For me, at the time and in light of the pride and entitlement I carried, this was devastating. I left a 10-year fast tracked military career and safety behind for a 'what if' opportunity. I was in my car going 100 MPH around the turn, watching in slow motion as I crept closer to the barrier, inch by inch. It would be over soon, I thought maybe it was too late to go back.

I had finished college, so I could have even rejoined the Army as an officer. In my self-pity, I needed a pick-me-up. At that time, a popular movie called, "Moneyball" was released (I won't explain it; everyone has seen it).

As I watched it and took it all in, something hit me differently. The nuances aside, the movie was about a quantitative system versus a qualitative one. What we learned and see in Major League Baseball today is that the quant system won. Suddenly, I realized where I was going wrong. I was modifying how I communicated after every interaction, based on the previous interaction I had.

The Problems I Faced:

- **Inconsistent Pitch:** Every time, my pitch was different. I was constantly changing my approach based on the last interaction.

- **Variable Requests:** Every time, I asked for something else, leading to confusion and inconsistency.

- **Manual Tallying:** I used tallies to count my knocks, but I sweated through them, making them hard to read.

- **Lost Contacts:** I lost contacts because of ink bleed or forgetting to write down the street name.

- **Lack of Clear Goals:** I stalled at the end because I didn't know what I wanted.

- **Time-Consuming 'Thank Yous':** I wasted tons of time handwriting 25-50 thank you cards a day.

- **No Sleep:** I got no sleep because I knocked from 8 to 8 and went to school at night.

- **Wasted Walking Time:** I wasted tons of time walking from door to door.

The Epiphany:

While watching "Moneyball," I saw the power of a quantitative, systematic approach. The idea that you could rely on data and a consistent system to achieve better results was a gamechanger for me.

The Shift:

I realized I needed to systematize my approach. Here's what I did to turn things around:

- **Standardized Pitch:** I developed a consistent pitch that I used every time, refining it based on data, not just gut feelings.

- **Consistent Requests:** I standardized my asks, making it clear and consistent what I needed from each interaction.

- **Digital Tracking:** I switched to a digital system for tracking my interactions, eliminating the problems with tallies and ink bleeds.

- **Clear Objectives:** I set clear goals for each interaction, so I always knew what the next step was.

- **Efficient Follow-Up:** I automated my 'thank you' notes and follow-ups, saving hours every day.

- **Balanced Schedule:** I created a balanced schedule that allowed for adequate rest and effective work hours.

- **Optimized Routes:** I planned my routes more efficiently to minimize walking time and maximize interactions.

The Results:

Implementing a systematic, quantitative approach transformed my effectiveness. I became more consistent, saved time, and achieved better results without burning out.

By learning from the "Moneyball" approach, I realized the power of data and consistency over intuition and guesswork. This shift not only improved my performance but also brought much-needed balance to my life.

In the midst of careening into a wall at 100mph, I punched it. No! I floored it. I took the next day off and built my system. I used lamination paper to waterproof my contact sheet and tri-folded it so that I could keep it in my back pocket, out of view, until it was time.

I wrote a new, simpler script. When knocking, I was constantly faced with objections that I didn't know how to handle, so I always left empty handed. I always handled, "I already have someone I work with" well because it didn't require much to answer. I built it into my script as a counterintuitive buoy for them to hit.

Have you ever been door-knocked? Most of the time, if you don't turn off the lights and pretend you aren't home, you answer because you mistook them for someone you knew or maybe an unfamiliar neighbor. When you realize it's just a knock, you want a way out ASAP, but it's not about the offer. As Americans, we're just weird about door-to-door people.

So, I sparked my first marketing fuse by building in the question at the end — "Are you currently working with anyone?" People couldn't answer fast enough. "Yes", "Yes sir", "yeppers", "all set here", "we got a guy that comes by every year at the company", "yeah my guy is…"

They were so happy; they didn't see what was coming. Instant deflation of their balloon. I knew they would say it, and I never missed a beat.

"Well, it's good you've got your money working for you, and like I mentioned, I'm just getting out, introducing myself to the community, as I'm about to expand my business this way. Once I get set up, would it be alright if I extended an invitation for you to come by, check out some seminars we'll be doing?" — Shut up.

Wearing sunglasses helped a lot with the awkward pause. Most of the time, they said, "Uh, okay, sure I guess…"

I'd say, "Great" and whip out my trifold contact sheet from my back pocket with a waterproof marker I had from the Army and commence my process.

"What's your first name? How do you spell your last? Area code 713, 281, or 832?" (they always say the full number).

Sometimes, people would stall here, knowing they didn't want to give out their number, sometimes even for uncomfortable amounts of time like 30-45 seconds. I never looked back up until they started saying the number or said "no", which was rare. By now, I could have left victorious

with my contact to input, but it wouldn't have helped me —
I had to get a financial need.

The Columbo Close

I'm too young to have watched Detective Columbo while
growing up, but my dad told me about this "Columbo" close
once at dinner (yeah, I was almost 30, living with my parents)
and thought it would be perfect to get my financial needs ID
with prospects. So, I added it in.

After I got the number (I wrote the address down after I left),
I would turn to start walking away, then stop quickly and
turn back to them and say, "Hey, I almost forgot... just so I
don't waste your time... if you had to say, retirement, saving
for college, or taxes, what is most important to you right
now?"

And just like that, business was booming. It felt like the scene
in Forrest Gump when the hurricane destroyed all the boats
except for Jenny, Bubba Gump Shrimp Company's prime
vessel. Except in my case, it was me scooping up numbers all
day, instead of shrimp.

I tweaked everything. I upgraded my tally system to a click
counter so it wouldn't get ruined and I wouldn't lose count.
I realized that 80% of my contacts came between 8am-10am
and 5pm-8pm; I only went out during those times. This

allowed me to do schoolwork in the afternoon or sometimes just float around in my parent's pool.

I was getting 30-40 legitimate, qualified leads daily. It became a game. By the end of summer, I had 746 leads. I went to my firm's home office in St. Louis, wondering how close the competition would be, and that's when I saw it:

J.L. Hohenstein – 746
Whoever – 258
Whoever – 196

What?! How did I smoke all these people? Because I punched it — I'm one of about 5 people from that class of over 100 still in financial services today. Thank God I did, because I'd be hating life if I went back into the military. But this isn't the last time using a system to find my way saved me. It happened again about 6 months in.

As it turned out, door knocking doesn't convert as well as phoning, and I sucked at it more than door knocking. Plus, it gave me massive anxiety. I would spend most of my time emailing until I worked up enough courage to run through 10 calls or so.

So, here I was, hundreds to call, without the courage to do it. I've literally fought another human to death with my bare hands and I couldn't pick up the phone. That pep talk wasn't helpful for me then either. I was doing okay, making it, until an opportunity came up.

It was an excuse to avoid making phone calls, so I signed up for an American Funds event featuring a remarkable speaker, Dr. Jason Selk. Dr. Selk is a renowned performance coach known for helping to mentally coach the St. Louis Cardinals to two World Series Championships. His expertise in mental toughness and performance optimization is legendary.

At the event, I discovered an approach called "Organize Tomorrow Today," championed by Tom Bartow, Dr. Selk, and some other guy. Since that day, I've integrated what I learned into my daily routine and continue to use it in various ways.

You should definitely check out the book, but here's how it works, and why all new people at our firm use it during their first year, regardless of their experience.

Concepts from Organize Tomorrow Today

1. **Win the Fight-Thru:** Identify your most important task (MIT) and complete it first thing in the morning. This helps you build momentum for the rest of the day. The idea is to tackle the task that is most likely to bring you closer to your goals.

2. **Dominate the Morning Routine:** Create a consistent morning routine that sets you up for

success. This might include exercise, meditation, or reviewing your goals. A strong morning routine can help you start the day with clarity and energy.

3. **Set Up Your Day the Night Before:** Plan your day the night before by listing your MITs for the next day. This reduces decision fatigue and ensures you start your day with a clear focus on what's important.

4. **Maximize the Power of 3:** Focus on completing three critical tasks each day. This prevents overwhelm and ensures you're always moving forward on your most important goals.

5. **Lean on Accountability Partners:** Share your goals and progress with a trusted colleague or mentor. Having someone to hold you accountable increases your commitment and helps you stay on track.

6. **Control Your Attention:** Practice focusing your attention on one task at a time. Multitasking reduces efficiency and increases stress. By controlling your attention, you can improve your productivity and the quality of your work.

7. **Develop a Mastery Mindset:** Focus on continuous improvement and learning. Approach your tasks with the goal of mastering them, rather than just completing them. This mindset helps you to grow and achieve higher levels of performance.

8. **Reflect and Refine:** At the end of each day, reflect on what you accomplished and identify areas for improvement. This reflection helps you to learn from your experiences and continuously refine your approach.

By incorporating these principles, you can structure your days for maximum efficiency and effectiveness. This approach not only boosts productivity but also reduces stress and increases job satisfaction.

Adopting the "Organize Tomorrow Today" method has been a gamechanger for me and my team. It provides a clear framework for achieving daily goals and maintaining a high level of performance. Give it a try and see how it transforms your workflow and results. Since originally adopting this, we've built and included meaningful ways to reflect and introspect on the journey, including adding a point-based system to make it more satisfying at the end.

As you can probably guess, this will absolutely help you hit the throttle every day. But if you aren't mindful of the fact that you are inescapably human, you will pay an enormous cost and you won't be able to sustain yourself for very long at an effective rate.

You could just "power" through it — many do. I did this myself for nearly a decade in the Army. I was one of the best — Decorated Combat Veteran, Olympic-level fitness, Crack

Shot… I won every award for leadership, did all the schools, never asked for help, never failed, never quit. I had a tangible track record of being able to kill other humans in various ways without even blinking.

I was turned into a machine and told I never needed to be anything else. I believed it with my all, but it came with a price. I had no real relationships. The facade I maintained with my wife was the only way to seem normal. I loved them but hated myself more.

I didn't sleep — maybe four hours a night. I woke up exhausted and covered it up with nicotine and caffeine. By the end of the day, I needed alcohol to sleep, but that ruined my sleep quality. I had an eating disorder from repeated stints in situations where I had to eat most of my calories in one sitting at the end of the day. The food was trash, so I covered that up with supplements and multivitamins.

I thought constantly about the faces of those who tried to take me from this earth and I helped them "board the plane" instead. Despite knowing how wrong it felt, I believed it was right — this contradiction haunted me.

Fortunately, this won't happen in financial services, but here's what will if you aren't careful:

- You'll convince yourself to trade everything for money — your time, your stress levels, being there for your family, etc.

- You'll promise that you'll trade it back when you "make it."

- You'll make it and then realize you're trapped because nearly all of your habits were built to kill you in order to make money.

- Change is hard. You probably missed most of the important stuff anyway. You dislike your spouse now because you both became different people, so you blame them and leave.

- To protect yourself, you'll switch your self-valuation to be about giving everyone money at the end, so they'll be okay.

- You'll keep doing what you've trained yourself your whole life to do — trade everything for money. Then you can avoid change but still feel good.

- You'll wonder why no one ever calls you despite all the money you've given them, or when they do — it's to ask for money.

Don't worry, I'm not clairvoyant in this respect. What I'm describing to you is men from the Baby Boomer generation and Generation X — pretty much most of them. As I write this, I can already think of 30 people, personal and clients, that took this journey.

Let's find a new path now, instead of trying to undo a lifetime of bad habits built by the ones who came before us. It comes from reflecting in a real way, not like what you're thinking — holding hands in a circle while someone prompts you to share. It's one-on-one, you-to-you. If you can't be honest with yourself, it's going to be hard to be honest with others.

You should never, ever, lie to yourself and believe it. It's like drinking poison. I'm not saying tell the truth all the time, no matter what (that's your choice), but it's very normal for a person to lie to avoid a consequence, big or small.

If you decide to do that, just make sure you don't believe your own bullshit. Lying to yourself and breaking promises to yourself are the two things that decrease self-confidence and self-esteem. You need both of those in spades for this to work (and to be happy).

Here's a framework to help you start — do it every day.

The key to this is building the habit, then improving the quality.

Daily Reflection Example

1. What did I achieve today?

2. What could I have done better?

3. Did I stay true to my values and goals?

4. What is my top priority for tomorrow?

This should start as soon as you begin this work. The answers can be simple at first. You can say you achieved nothing, everything could be better, no you weren't true to your values, and you have no clue what your top priority is tomorrow. This isn't a test; it's a habit that you're building. Like I said earlier, in order to be good at anything, you have to suck at it first.

10

EMBRACE AND LEVERAGE AI

For those who know me, you'll know that I saved my favorite topic for last— AI.

The first thing here is, if you are afraid of this, know that it's because you've been told to be and you believe you should be. But that ends now. AI is here to stay, so let's understand how what we know as Artificial Intelligence is really Assisted Intelligence.

Understanding GPT Models

GPT models work by processing vast amounts of text data to predict and generate human-like responses. They don't "think" like humans but are extremely good at recognizing patterns and making educated guesses based on the data they've been trained on.

Assisted Intelligence vs. Artificial Intelligence

While true Artificial General Intelligence (AGI) is still on the horizon, what we have now is more like Assisted Intelligence. Current AI operates in what's known as "Parrot" mode — repeating and recombining information it has learned, without true understanding of consciousness.

What AI Can Do Now

Even in its current state, AI has some incredible capabilities:

- **Infinite Processing Speed:** AI can process information infinitely faster than a human brain.

- **Vast Knowledge Base:** AI has access to more information than any individual could ever learn.

- **Pattern Recognition:** AI recognizes patterns and associations at lightning speed.

- **Enhanced Memory:** AI has better short-term and long-term memory capabilities compared to humans.

- **Typing Speed:** AI can generate text 1,000 times faster than a human can type.

- **Advanced Inference:** AI can make inferences and connections much faster and more accurately than a human.

The AI Brain

What does that sound like? It sounds like a brain that traded feelings, thoughts, and emotions for infinite informational and computational power. By understanding these capabilities, you can leverage AI as a powerful tool to assist you in your work, enhancing your productivity and decision-making. We don't have to choose, *we get both.*

So, from here forward, we are aligning to the possibility that you can, in fact, have two brains, or perhaps, a 2-stage brain — one in your body, full of memories, emotions, love, and all the work we've done to come to life, and one out of your body, full of information, computational power, and process agility.

This is the world we're entering — where the professionals who become million/billionaires are the ones who become the masters of the extensions.

Here's what I mean.

Imagine a contest with a panel of CPAs, attorneys, and advisors at one table, and me with my extended brain at the other. 100 people take turns to ask questions until there are 100 questions to answer. I guarantee that not only do I answer all these questions faster, but my answers are also way more accurate. It's got nothing to do with me — I was probably daydreaming as the questions got asked, and I don't give a shit.

A true message is always true regardless of the messenger. The panel accessed a faulty information system with competing priorities, prone to error as it attempts to uncover hidden information. I accessed a predictive information system with no competing priorities and infinite computing power that rarely makes errors as it unlocks relevant information to expand output.

The master guide of the future embraces and leverages this fact. Those who don't will be crushed — not by AI, but by people using AI. An end that is infinitely scarier than AI by itself.

Detailed and Highly Actionable Prompts for Financial Advisors Using AI

So, what can this extension of you do with substantially less work? Here are detailed and actionable prompts for each task:

1. **Write and Respond to Emails in Your Voice**
   - Prompt: "As a financial advisor, draft an email responding to a client's inquiry about portfolio diversification, maintaining my professional tone and style."

○ Prompt: "Compose a follow-up email to a prospective client who attended last week's webinar, encouraging them to schedule a consultation."

2. **Create Custom LinkedIn Messages Based on User Profiles**

   ○ Prompt: "Generate a personalized LinkedIn message for a potential client who is a recent retiree, highlighting how our services can help manage their retirement funds."

   ○ Prompt: "Write a LinkedIn connection request message to a local business owner, mentioning mutual connections and suggesting a coffee meeting to discuss potential financial strategies."

3. **Framework, Outline, and Build Webinars**

   ○ Prompt: "Outline a 60-minute webinar for financial advisors on the topic of tax-efficient investing, including key points, slides, and interactive elements."

   ○ Prompt: "Create a detailed framework for a webinar aimed at educating young professionals about the benefits of starting early with retirement planning.

4. **Write Daily Blog Posts**

   ○ Prompt: "Write a 500-word blog post on the current state of the stock market and its implications for long-term investors."

   ○ Prompt: "Draft a blog post offering tips for small business owners to manage their cash flow effectively."

5. **Check Content for Compliance**

   ○ Prompt: "Review the attached investment strategy document to ensure it complies with SEC regulations and guidelines."

   ○ Prompt: "Check the compliance of a newsletter draft that discusses retirement planning strategies."

6. **Craft White Papers**

   ○ Prompt: "Draft a comprehensive white paper on the benefits and risks of alternative investments for high-net-worth individuals."

   ○ Prompt: "Create a white paper on the impact of global economic trends on local investment opportunities."

7. **Design and Framework Brochures**

   ○ Prompt: "Design a brochure outlining our financial planning services, including sections for retirement planning, wealth management, and tax strategies."

- o Prompt: "Create a framework for a brochure targeting young professionals, focusing on the importance of early financial planning."

8. **Develop a 30-Day Social Media Strategy**

- o Prompt: "Develop a 30-day social media strategy for promoting our new retirement planning services, including daily posts, engagement tactics, and performance metrics."

- o Prompt: "Create a content calendar for the next month focused on educating clients about the benefits of diversified portfolios."

9. **Generate Headlines and Bullet Points**

- o Prompt: "Generate compelling headlines and bullet points for a landing page promoting our financial advisory services."

- o Prompt: "Create headlines and key takeaways for an email campaign targeting potential clients interested in wealth management."

10. **Draft High-Value Content**

- o Prompt: "Write a detailed guide on how to create a balanced investment portfolio for long-term growth."

- Prompt: "Draft an article on the top five financial mistakes retirees should avoid."

11. **Design Email Campaigns and Sequences**

    - Prompt: "Design a 5-email sequence for new clients, introducing them to our services and the benefits of working with us."

    - Prompt: "Create an email campaign to re-engage past clients, offering them a complimentary portfolio review."

12. **Comparatively Analyze Two Portfolios (Qualitative and Quantitative)**

    - Prompt: "Compare and contrast two investment portfolios, analyzing their risk, return, and asset allocation."

    - Prompt: "Provide a qualitative and quantitative analysis of a client's current portfolio versus a proposed alternative."

13. **Write Monthly Market Updates**

    - Prompt: "Write a monthly market update summarizing key economic events, market trends, and investment opportunities."

    - Prompt: "Draft a market update focusing on the impact of recent interest rate changes on various asset classes."

14. Summarize Recent Economic Events

- ○ Prompt: "Summarize the key points from the latest Federal Reserve meeting and its implications for investors."

- ○ Prompt: "Provide a summary of recent geopolitical events and their potential impact on global markets."

15. Teach You More About Your Role

- ○ Prompt: "Explain the role of a financial advisor in estate planning, including key responsibilities and best practices."

- ○ Prompt: "Provide an overview of the latest regulatory changes affecting financial advisors."

16. Optimize Financial Plans

- ○ Prompt: "Review and optimize a financial plan for a client aiming to retire in 10 years, focusing on maximizing returns and minimizing risks."

- ○ Prompt: "Evaluate a financial plan for tax efficiency and suggest improvements."

17. Quickly Check Portfolios for Issues

- ○ Prompt: "Quickly analyze a client's portfolio for any potential issues or red flags."

- Prompt: "Identify areas of concern in a portfolio that might require rebalancing."

18. **Create Competitive Assessments**

    - Prompt: "Create a competitive assessment comparing our services to those of top competitors in the financial advisory industry."

    - Prompt: "Evaluate the strengths and weaknesses of a competitor's financial product offerings."

19. **Build Investment Policy Statements**

    - Prompt: "Draft an investment policy statement for a new client, outlining their investment goals, risk tolerance, and asset allocation strategy."

    - Prompt: "Create an investment policy statement for a corporate client, focusing on long-term growth and sustainability."

20. **Identify Gaps in Your Events or Funnels**

    - Prompt: "Analyze our current marketing funnel and identify gaps where potential clients are dropping off."

    - Prompt: "Review the event planning process for our seminars and suggest improvements to increase attendance and engagement."

21. Enhance Aspects of Your Character

- ○ Prompt: "Develop a plan to enhance your public speaking skills for client presentations."

- ○ Prompt: "Identify ways to improve your networking abilities to build stronger client relationships."

22. Build Avatars for Ads

- ○ Prompt: "Create detailed client avatars for our ad campaigns, focusing on demographics, interests, and financial needs."

- ○ Prompt: "Develop personas for potential clients in different age groups for targeted advertising."

23. Assess Competitor Websites

- ○ Prompt: "Evaluate a competitor's website, highlighting strengths and areas where our site could improve."

- ○ Prompt: "Compare the user experience of our website to that of a leading competitor."

24. Summarize Books and Concepts

- ○ Prompt: "Summarize the key concepts from 'The Intelligent Investor' by Benjamin Graham and explain how they apply to modern investing."

- Prompt: "Provide a summary of recent financial research on retirement planning strategies."

25. Rewrite Your Content

- Prompt: "Rewrite the content of our services page to make it more engaging and client-focused."

- Prompt: "Revise our company's mission statement to better reflect our values and goals."

26. Generate Ideas

- Prompt: "Generate ideas for a series of educational workshops for our clients."

- Prompt: "Brainstorm new topics for our monthly newsletter to keep our clients informed and engaged."

Imagine everything you'd need to study or learn to do this well and how long it would take. With AI, you don't have to. It's only getting better; AI is our friend.

Real Use Cases

Easy Use Cases:

1. Daily Email Management: AI drafts and responds to emails, freeing up hours of your day.

2. Content Creation: Write blog posts or social media updates effortlessly.

3. Portfolio Checkups: Quickly analyze investment portfolios for issues or improvements.

4. Market Updates: Get concise summaries of recent economic events to stay informed.

Cool Use Cases:

1. Webinar Development: AI frameworks and outlines a webinar tailored to your audience.

2. Social Media Strategy: Develop a 30-day social media campaign that targets your key demographics.

3. White Papers and Reports: AI drafts in-depth reports and white papers with minimal input.

4. Character Enhancement: AI helps you refine and enhance your personal and professional traits.

Custom GPT Frameworks

Basic GPT Prompt Frameworks:

1. **[Expert Role] [Task] [Action]**
   o Example: "As a financial advisor, draft an email to a client explaining the benefits of a diversified portfolio."

2. [Problem] [Solution] [Outcome]

   ○ Example: "Explain how investing in index funds can mitigate risk and lead to steady returns over time."

3. [Audience] [Need] [Content Type]

   ○ Example: "For recent college graduates, create a blog post about managing student loan debt."

4. [Topic] [Context] [Output]

   ○ Example: "Discuss the impact of interest rate changes on the housing market in a detailed report."

5. [Scenario] [Objective] [Deliverable]

   ○ Example: "In a market downturn, outline strategies to protect investments in a presentation."

6. [Task] [Tool] [Result]

   ○ Example: "Using technical analysis, identify potential buy signals for a stock."

7. [Role] [Request] [Format]

   ○ Example: "As a marketing manager, create a social media campaign plan in a PDF document."

8. **[Goal] [Challenge] [Advice]**

   ○ Example: "For a small business owner, offer advice on improving cash flow during a slow season."

Bot Framework

If you find yourself constantly doing the same things with AI, it might be time to create a custom worker GPT or "bot." Here's a simple framework to build them:

1. **Identify Repetitive Tasks:**

   ○ List the tasks you frequently perform that could be automated.

2. **Define the Bot's Role:**

   ○ Clearly define what the bot is supposed to do.

   ○ Example: "Customer Support Bot for answering common questions."

3. **Create Prompt Templates:**

   ○ Use the basic GPT frameworks to create prompt templates.

   ○ Example: "As a [Role], [Action] to achieve [Outcome]."

4. **Set Up Workflow:**

   ○ Design the workflow the bot will follow.

- Example: "Receive inquiry > Identify question type > Generate response > Send response."

5. **Test and Refine:**

   - Run tests to ensure the bot performs as expected and make necessary adjustments.

6. **Implement and Monitor:**

   - Deploy the bot in your workflow and monitor its performance regularly.

   - Example: "Monitor response accuracy and user satisfaction."

Custom GPT Prompts

GPT Specifically Trained to Help Expand Your Hero's Avatar

- **Prompt:** "Create a detailed hero avatar for a financial advisor, targeting young professionals starting their first job, including demographics, psychographics, goals, and pain points."

- **Prompt:** "Expand the hero avatar for a financial advisor focused on helping retirees, detailing their financial concerns, lifestyle aspirations, and key motivations."

GPT Specifically Trained to Help Improve Your Story

- **Prompt:** "Analyze and enhance my personal story as a financial advisor, focusing on my journey, challenges, and triumphs to better connect with potential clients."

- **Prompt:** "Improve the storytelling of my brand's origin, highlighting key moments and lessons learned to create a compelling narrative."

GPT Specifically Trained to Help Improve Your Mousetrap

- **Prompt:** "Evaluate my current lead generation strategy (mousetrap) and provide actionable suggestions to increase effectiveness and conversion rates."

- **Prompt:** "Optimize my sales funnel (mousetrap) for attracting high-net-worth clients, identifying any gaps and suggesting improvements."

GPT Specifically Trained to Help Improve Your Reflections/Level It Up into a Coach

- **Prompt:** "Provide a structured daily reflection routine to help me assess my performance as a financial advisor, including key questions to ask myself."

- **Prompt:** "Act as a virtual coach and offer guidance on how to improve my client interaction skills and overall professional development."

GPT Blog Factory

- **Prompt:** "Generate a series of blog post ideas for a financial advisor targeting millennials, focusing on relevant financial topics and trends."

- **Prompt:** "Write a detailed blog post on the benefits of Roth IRAs for young professionals, including statistics and actionable advice."

GPT Post Factory

- **Prompt:** "Create a month's worth of social media posts for a financial advisor, including images, captions, and hashtags, aimed at increasing engagement and attracting new clients."

- **Prompt:** "Draft engaging LinkedIn posts that showcase client success stories and the impact of effective financial planning."

GPT Event Planner

- **Prompt:** "Plan a virtual seminar for financial advisors on the topic of retirement planning, including an agenda, speaker suggestions, and promotional strategies."

- **Prompt:** "Develop a detailed plan for a client appreciation event, including venue recommendations, activities, and a follow-up strategy."

If this seems like a lot, you're exploring a way of acting and thinking that's very foreign to you — so it's supposed to. Remember, this is the hard path that practically guarantees your success. There are lots of other easy books you can read to ensure you're back here in 6 months if you wish. The reason for that is, this book is about knowing what you need to do, and doing it, not about learning something you will forget later, just to say "yeah, I read that book; it was okay".

I'd rather you give this to someone who will act upon it than for it to sit on your bookshelf as a trophy of accumulated knowledge. This is because I'm secretly creating a powerful movement of next level financial advisors that will one day manage nearly all of the world's wealth.

They'll do it by transforming themselves with this book. So, if you don't take action, it is a promise to you that others will and clients will see their lights shining and go towards them and away from you. It is the mission of time, it is the mission of time, it is the mission of time.

I call you now, Hero, to accept this challenge; it's why you have come. If you deny it, know that you are still loved. We know who you are. When we find you again, not in your light, we will remind you of what you are. When you see us and attempt to hide, we will shine the light on you and remind you of how you serve. This change is already underway and will happen much faster and sooner than you think.

I know *who* you are.

I know *what* you are.

I know *how* you serve.

Now, you do too, and you may never not know this again — regardless of your choice.

#Bonus Content - Recommended Gear:

As you continue on this journey, you will have to level up. Some of the most important aspects of your digital brand revolve around how you show up online. If you behave like my parents or people's grandparents whose faces are cut in half when they talk on a low pixel video, please stop. You are ruining 100% of your credibility. If you're older and work with younger people, they are 100% going to make fun of you for this, and that is not a powerful guide.

For recommended gear, I offer the following, and I'm too lazy to do affiliate QR codes just to try to make money off of you. So, just google them and check them out for yourself:

For Video: The only webcam I recommend is the **Insta360 Link** webcam. The reason for this is that it has an AI tracking swivel mount to follow your face and always keep you center stage, it has other modes like whiteboard mode and "draw on the table" mode. It has a 1.7 depth of field which creates a nice natural blur effect without the choppy outlines done automatically by software like Zoom and similar platforms. It's very lightweight and compact for use and travel; I go *everywhere* with my webcam. It also has a built-in audio capture if you're in a pinch. Pound-for-pound, it is the most versatile webcam out there for financial advisors. You can check them out at https://www.insta360.com/

For Audio: For audio capture, which I would argue is the most important aspect of being online, I only use **Shure Audio Devices**. For my home office and studio, it's exclusively the **Shure SMB7** and when I travel or do podcast recordings, etc, with other people, I have them use my **Shure MV7**. You can find both on https://www.shure.com

For Recording Tools: I typically use dual recordings, so I have more options later on how to use the recordings. I do this automatically through **Zoom** where I hold my meeting, and I have a backup recording going with **Loom**. We'll call it the Zoom & Loom set up. By doing this, I have cloud-based recordings with attendees on deck for compliance submissions and follow ups. Additionally, my Loom recordings are auto-transcribed, auto-edited, and I can do things like add comments to them. This redundancy helps in my post-production process, since I don't outsource it (most people suck at it or make it really spammy-looking). I also use Loom to send explainers to people. For example, if a client wants to know how to find something unrelated to financial or personal data, like a website feature, I'll use the video to craft a personal explanation for them, thereby elevating my client experience.

For Content Creation: For financial advisors who need quick designs with high quality and lots of assets to differentiate their brand, Canva is the primary option to help you. It has everything you need to create almost any piece of content you could ever want, and with the use of brand kits, you can consistently create content quickly. In addition to this, you can even take slide decks and upload them to transform them into whitepapers and other things. Canva has heavy adoption of AI and will only continue these improvements as time goes on. You can learn more at www.canva.com. For more experienced designers or if it becomes a hobby, you can upgrade yourself to Figma which has a more robust platform and you can even design your websites, or aspects of your website. You can learn more about it at www.figma.com.

For Websites: If you're able to create your own website and not forced to be some generic person on a huge corporate website, then you need to do this. Pretty much any "financial advisor" website builder is a no-go. They'll sell you on how easy it is to use and makes compliance a cinch, but the reality is what you gain in ease of compliance, you pretty much lose everywhere else. For beginner web-builders, use the combo with **Wordpress** and **Elementor**. You can get the bundle for less than $200 per year at https://elementor.com/wordpress-hosting/ It includes hooking up to the Cloudflare Content Delivery Network (CDN), which is the fastest platform to deliver your site. It's unrivaled for the price. When you're ready to scale up and stand toe-to-toe with major financial services websites, use Wordpress because even the best financial services marketers are still beginners in the broader context of marketing. For this, you'll want to work with a developer to craft a custom site on **Webflow** which is absolutely the future of website building. Where **Wordpress** requires use of code-heavy plug-ins for automation and integration purposes, **Webflow** has the plug-ins coded directly into the website using the most modern approaches to code mark ups. I understand that this might sound like gibberish, but just know this is an evolving game.

I'll stop here with this list since the intent is for the book to be evergreen with updatable bonus sections, and giving you too much will overwhelm you. Just remember that you joined a profession with unlimited income potential, which requires an entrepreneurial spirit to succeed. You must adopt a mindset of "lifelong learner" because that's what you'll need to do to stay ahead of the curve.

You can become a dinosaur if you wish and keep everything the same because you're comfortable, but it's only a matter of time before the people who did read this book and take action come for your clients in the most loving way possible.

Bonus Content - AI Resources (2024):

For the record, I have not tried all of these tools and they do not come as recommendations from me other than the ones I have noted with the asterisk (*) symbol. In any instance, it's important to know that there are tools out there that can rapidly accelerate your and your team's work. These will become obsolete and replaced by more advanced models

- **ChatGPT by OpenAI**: Ideal for content creation, client communication, brainstorming ideas, and drafting emails or reports. I have custom bots for specific purposes you can use for free below:
  - Email Optimization: https://chatgpt.com/g-fAgyVTbWF-email-parrot
  - Content Creation: https://chatgpt.com/g-hb0U6YyVj-zebra-lead-magnets
  - Business Development Ideas: https://chatgpt.com/g-okqsWZIqS-fox-prospector
  - Advisor Guidance & Learning: https://chatgpt.com/g-G4nlyqanu-advisor-owl

- Social Posting & Strategy: https://chatgpt.com/g/g-CBX0z8pMZ-post-peacock

- LinkedIn Profile & Messaging: https://chatgpt.com/g/g-wb6KqwmO5-network-octopus

- **Promee.AI***: This is my personal, custom-built, web-based software for financial advisors. It's designed to handle all of your content needs from end-to-end. If you're creating something that uses words, then this is the program for you. But I'm a little biased, so check it out and see for yourself. Learn more at www.promee.ai

- **Canva**: Useful for creating visually appealing marketing materials, social media graphics, and presentations.

- **Klapp.App**: A video repurposing tool that takes full-length videos and breaks them into smaller, optimal clips, complete with captions, subtitles, and even posting guidelines and hashtags.

- **Buffer**: Another excellent tool for social media scheduling, analytics, and engagement.

- **Zapier/Make**: Automates workflows by connecting different apps and services, saving time on repetitive tasks.

- **WordStream**: Helps with managing and optimizing online advertising campaigns, especially on Google Ads and social media.

- **Salesforce**: A powerful CRM platform that integrates AI to provide insights, manage client relationships, and streamline workflows.

- **Grammarly**: Enhances writing by offering grammar, punctuation, and style suggestions, ensuring professional communication.

- **Mailchimp**: An email marketing platform that uses AI to optimize campaigns, segment audiences, and track performance.

- **Ulinc**: Offers automated Linkedin sequence messaging, but requires someone who already has access to the platform to refer you in.

- **AdRoll**: Specializes in retargeting and display advertising, leveraging AI to optimize ad performance.

- **Clearbit**: Enriches CRM data with real-time company and contact information, enhancing client insights and prospecting.

- **Calendly***: Automates meeting scheduling, integrates with calendars, and offers AI-based meeting analytics.

- **Sniply**: Adds call-to-action overlays on shared content, driving traffic back to your site and generating leads.

- **Crystal***: Provides personality insights based on social media profiles, helping advisors tailor their communication styles.

- **BuzzSumo***: Identifies trending content and key influencers in the industry, aiding in content creation and outreach strategies.

- **Beautiful.ai***: An AI-powered presentation tool that helps create visually appealing and professional slide decks quickly and easily.

- **Slidesgo**: Uses AI to provide templates and design suggestions for creating impactful presentations.

- **Tome**: An AI-powered storytelling tool that assists in creating interactive presentations and pitch decks.

- **Otter.ai**: Provides AI-powered transcription services for meetings, interviews, and presentations, making it easier to create content from spoken word.

- **Phrasee**: Uses AI to generate and optimize email subject lines and marketing copy, increasing engagement rates.

- **Crayon***: An AI-driven competitive intelligence platform that tracks competitors' activities and provides actionable insights.

- **MarketMuse***: Uses AI to help optimize content for SEO, ensuring it ranks well on search engines and reaches the target audience.

- **Grain**: AI-powered tool to capture and summarize key moments in video calls, making it easier to share insights and create content from meetings.

- **Headlime**: An AI-powered copywriting tool that helps create engaging headlines, ads, emails, and more.

- **Turing**: AI-powered platform for sourcing and managing remote developers, helping streamline hiring and project management processes.

- **Fireflies.ai**: An AI-powered meeting assistant that records, transcribes, and analyzes voice conversations to create notes and action items.

- **QuillBot***: Uses AI to paraphrase and summarize text, making it useful for creating concise content and reports.

- **InVideo**: An AI-powered video creation tool that helps create professional-quality videos for marketing and social media.

Call To Action

Ready to take your financial practice to the next level? Scan the QR code below to access exclusive resources, marketing tools, and join a community of like-minded professionals committed to growth and excellence.

Unlock Proven Marketing Secrets: Discover the exact strategies top financial advisors use to consistently attract high-value clients and grow their businesses, even in competitive markets.

Connect with Industry Leaders: Gain insider access to a network of financial experts and thought leaders who will share their insights and help you stay ahead of industry trends.

Receive Tailored Action Plans: Get personalized guidance and step-by-step action plans designed to address your unique challenges and accelerate your path to success.

Don't miss out on the opportunity to elevate your practice and achieve the success you've always envisioned.

Scan now and start your journey towards becoming an unstoppable force in the financial services industry!

ABOUT THE AUTHOR

Josh has always been driven by a deep desire to understand the mechanisms that drive the world and use them to create transformative change. After serving in the military, he transitioned into the financial services industry in 2016, armed with securities and insurance licenses and a relentless work ethic. Despite a rocky start, which included doorknocking in the sweltering streets of Houston and facing numerous rejections and even dangers, Josh's tenacity and perseverance never wavered.

His journey has been anything but easy. From being chased by dogs and having guns pulled on him while his shoes melted to the pavement, to facing the devastation of Hurricane Harvey, Josh's resilience has been tested time and again. Yet, these challenges only strengthened his resolve to succeed and make a meaningful impact in the lives of those he serves. His stint in disaster relief and recovery, where he navigated the complexities of non-profit marketing, further honed his skills and deepened his understanding of human connection and community support.

Returning to financial services with renewed vigor, Josh embraced innovative marketing techniques and leveraged technology to grow his practice. His unique approach, blending empathy with cutting-edge strategies, has helped him build authentic client relationships and a thriving practice.

Today, Josh is a beacon of inspiration for financial advisors and professionals. He combines his extensive industry knowledge with a heartfelt commitment to guiding others on their path to success. His writing offers insights that can revolutionize how financial services are delivered and experienced, focusing on practical strategies and personal growth.

In his downtime, Josh enjoys testing new marketing theories, experimenting with AI, and continuously exploring creative strategies to enhance the way humans connect. His story is a testament to the power of perseverance, innovation, and a genuine desire to help others succeed.